AF608600

Julia Neumeyer

Malta and the European Union

A small island state and its way into a powerful community

AN INTERDISCIPLINARY SERIES
OF THE CENTRE FOR INTERCULTURAL AND EUROPEAN STUDIES

INTERDISZIPLINÄRE SCHRIFTENREIHE
DES CENTRUMS FÜR INTERKULTURELLE UND EUROPÄISCHE STUDIEN

CINTEUS ▪ Fulda University of Applied Sciences ▪ Hochschule Fulda

ISSN 1865-2255

1 *Julia Neumeyer*
Malta and the European Union
A small island state and its way into a powerful community
ISBN 978-389821-814-6

Series Editors

Gudrun Hentges
Volker Hinnenkamp
Anne Honer
Hans-Wolfgang Platzer

Fachbereich Sozial- und Kulturwissenschaften
Hochschule Fulda University of Applied Sciences
Marquardstraße 35
D-36039 Fulda

cinteus@sk.hs-fulda.de
www.cinteus.eu

Julia Neumeyer

MALTA AND THE EUROPEAN UNION

A small island state and its way into a powerful community

ibidem-Verlag
Stuttgart

Bibliografische Information der Deutschen Nationalbibliothek
Die Deutsche Nationalbibliothek verzeichnet diese Publikation in der Deutschen Nationalbibliografie; detaillierte bibliografische Daten sind im Internet über http://dnb.d-nb.de abrufbar.

Bibliographic information published by the Deutsche Nationalbibliothek
Die Deutsche Nationalbibliothek lists this publication in the Deutsche Nationalbibliografie; detailed bibliographic data are available in the Internet at http://dnb.d-nb.de.

∞

Gedruckt auf alterungsbeständigem, säurefreien Papier
Printed on acid-free paper

ISBN-10: 3-89821-814-7

ISBN-13: 978-3-89821-814-6

© *ibidem*-Verlag
Stuttgart 2007

Alle Rechte vorbehalten

Das Werk einschließlich aller seiner Teile ist urheberrechtlich geschützt. Jede Verwertung außerhalb der engen Grenzen des Urheberrechtsgesetzes ist ohne Zustimmung des Verlages unzulässig und strafbar. Dies gilt insbesondere für Vervielfältigungen, Übersetzungen, Mikroverfilmungen und elektronische Speicherformen sowie die Einspeicherung und Verarbeitung in elektronischen Systemen.

All rights reserved. No part of this publication may be reproduced, stored in or introduced into a retrieval system, or transmitted, in any form, or by any means (electronical, mechanical, photocopying, recording or otherwise) without the prior written permission of the publisher. Any person who does any unauthorized act in relation to this publication may be liable to criminal prosecution and civil claims for damages.

Printed in Germany

Editorial

This series is intended as a publication panel of the Centre of Intercultural and European Studies (CINTEUS) at Fulda University of Applied Sciences. The series aims at making research results, anthologies, conference readers, study books and selected qualification theses accessible to the general public. It comprises of scientific and interdisciplinary works on inter- and transculturality; the European Union from an interior and a global perspective; and problems of social welfare and social law in Europe. Each of these are fields of research and teaching in the Social- and Cultural Studies Faculty at Fulda University of Applied Sciences and its Centre for Intercultural and European Studies. We also invite contributions from outside the faculty that share and enrich our research.

Gudrun Hentges, Volker Hinnenkamp, Anne Honer & Hans-Wolfgang Platzer

Editorial

Die Buchreihe versteht sich als Publikationsforum des Centrums für interkulturelle und europäische Studien (CINTEUS) der Hochschule Fulda. Ziel der CINTEUS-Reihe ist es, Forschungsergebnisse, Anthologien, Kongressreader, Studienbücher und ausgewählte Qualifikationsarbeiten einer interessierten Öffentlichkeit zugänglich zu machen. Die Reihe umfasst fachwissenschaftliche und interdisziplinäre Arbeiten aus den Bereichen Inter- und Transkulturalität, Europäische Union aus Binnen- und globaler Perspektive sowie wohlfahrtsstaatliche und sozialrechtliche Probleme Europas. All dies sind Fachgebiete, die im Fachbereich Sozial- und Kulturwissenschaften der Hochschule Fulda University of Applied Sciences und dem angegliederten Centrum für interkulturelle und Europastudien gelehrt und erforscht werden. Ausdrücklich eingeladen an der Publikationsreihe mitzuwirken sind auch solche Studien, die nicht 'im Hause' entstanden sind, aber CINTEUS-Schwerpunkte berühren und bereichern.

Gudrun Hentges, Volker Hinnenkamp, Anne Honer & Hans-Wolfgang Platzer

Vorwort zum vorliegenden Band

Die vorliegende Studie über Maltas Weg in die Europäische Union, mit der diese Schriftenreihe eröffnet wird, leistet im Bereich der Europaforschung ein Zweifaches:

Zum einen bietet diese Studie für einen an integrationswissenschaftlichen Fragen interessierten Leserkreis eine theoriegeleitete Analyse, die unter dem Blickwinkel der „Außenpolitik kleiner Länder“ den schwierigen Weges dieses Inselstaates in die Europäische Union nachzeichnet und sorgfältig interpretiert.

Zum anderen gelingt es Julia Neumeyer ein in der öffentlichen wie wissenschaftlichen Wahrnehmung bislang eher vernachlässigtes neues EU-Mitgliedsland in profunder Weise zu porträtieren. Für einen an politischer Landeskunde interessierten Leserkreis bietet diese Monografie damit zugleich auf knappem Raum eine empirisch fundierte Einführung in die politischen Strukturen und sozialökonomischen Entwicklungen Maltas.

Hans-Wolfgang Platzer

Acknowledgements

Writing this paper was a unique experience for me. Immersing myself into this exciting topic broadened my horizons about this fascinating Mediterranean island. The idea to write about Malta and the European Union came to me during an internship at *Malta Enterprise* in San Gwann, Malta. During my stay in Malta, I gained an insight into the island's turbulent history and its rich culture. I was given a unique opportunity to learn about Malta's political and economic institutions and organisations. Back in Germany, months of intensive research and many weeks of writing rendered my Malta-project complete, which I would not have managed without the help of many supporters. I would like to thank Dr Stefanie Anzinger for offering me the internship placement at *Malta Enterprise* and for her support during my stay. Thanks to Brigitte Tanti from the *Euro Info Centre*, Malta, who showed me around the Centre's library and provided me with valuable literature. My thanks also go to Victoria Azzopardi from the Bank of Valletta for promptly sending me hardcopies of articles from the *Bank of Valletta Review* at no cost.

I would like to express my gratitude to Prof. Dr. Hans-Wolfgang Platzer and Prof. Dr. Gudrun Hentges, whose expertise and understanding have added considerably to finalising my study.

Joany Grima, dear friend from Malta, thank you for your invaluable contributions and comments.

A special thanks goes to my parents for their support and encouragement.

Finally, I would also especially like to thank Torsten for his creative support, motivating feedback and patience.

August 2006 Julia Neumeyer

Contents

Editorial 5

Vorwort zum vorliegenden Band 7

Acknowledgements 9

Contents 11

1. Introduction 13

2. Malta – Key factors and figures 17

3. Theoretical framework 19

3.1. Theories of European Integration 20

3.2. Foreign Policy Approaches 25

3.2.1 Neorealism 25

3.2.2. Utilitarian Liberalism 27

3.2.3. Constructivism 28

3.3. Small State Theory 31

3.3.1. Difficulties in defining “smallness” 33

3.3.2. Problems and strategies of small states 36

3.3.3. Small states’ foreign policy behaviour 40

4. Development of Malta-EU relations 43

4.1. After Malta’s Independence: orientation and deterioration 43

4.2. Malta’s political culture and party system 47

4.3. 1984 to 1992: Back on the road towards EU membership 50

4.4. 1993 to 1999: Two Commission’s opinions and two elections 55

4.5. Alternatives to EU membership 60

4.5.1. European integration or Mediterranean collaboration? 61

4.5.2. Free Trade Area Agreement or Customs Union 62

4.6. 1999 to 2004: Negotiations, Referendum and Accession Process 65

5. EU membership: Economic and Political Considerations 77

6. Accession Treaty and Representation in EU institutions 83
7. Malta in the EU: Issue of Smallness & Political Priorities 85
7.1. Large states versus small states in an Enlarged Union? 85
7.2. Malta's Priority Agendas as EU Member 90
7.2.1. Foreign Policy Agenda 90
7.2.2. Domestic Priorities 93
8. Conclusion 97
References 101
Official EU documents 107
Internet sources 108
Malta Government Documents 108
Other Internet Sources 109
Appendix: List of Abbreviations 111

1. Introduction

On May 1 2004 the European Union accomplished an event, best described as one of the major landmarks in the long standing history of European integration. On this day, following the signing of the Accession Treaty on April 16 2003 in Athens and the completion of the ratification process, ten new member states with a combined population of almost 75 million officially joined the EU. The new members were three former Soviet republics Estonia, Latvia and Lithuania, four former satellites of the USSR being Poland, the Czech Republic, Hungary and Slovakia, the former Yugoslav republic Slovenia and the two Mediterranean islands Cyprus and Malta.[1]

This fifth enlargement was remarkable in various respects. It was not only the biggest expansion ever faced by the EU, but it was also an enlargement round very different in character from those previous. The number of EU member states almost doubled from 15 to 25 with Bulgaria and Romania already awaiting to join in 2007. The new countries are very different from the "old" EU 15 member states and differ in many aspects from each other.[2] Is the European Union able to manage such a unique situation in an adequate way? What are the political consequences? Which institutional problems does this historical step entail? What are the economic opportunities and difficulties linked to enlargement? Such questions have been posed and extensively analysed in the run-up to accession and are still widely discussed topics in Europe. Countless books and articles evaluating the European Union's strategy in coping with the accession and discussing the effects which the enlargement has on the "old" members have been published. The common focal point among them is primarily on the European Union, rather than the specific situation of each accession country.[3]

---

[1] http://europa.eu.int/scadplus/leg/en/lvb/e50017.htm

[2] Differences exist for example in their respective political and economic situation in comparison to the "old member states". This issue cannot be discussed in greater detail here, because of the limited scope of the thesis. For more information see for example Nugent (2003), 494 ff.; Grabbe; Kreile in Weidenfeld (2004).

[3] See for example the contributions in Hall (2000).

The integration of the ten new member states has been portrayed as "the culmination of a long accession process leading to the reunification of a Europe that had been divided for half a century by the Iron Curtain and the Cold War".[4] This statement indicates the centre of attention is particularly directed towards the post-communist countries in Central and Eastern Europe. Hence, in the media and literature the expansion of the EU is often termed "Eastern Enlargement" according to the geographical position of these countries and their striking role in the European integration process. The Mediterranean countries Cyprus and Malta, which are also part of the enlargement process, are either not included or, for the sake of completeness, mentioned in just a few words. It might be assumed that Cyprus and Malta do not receive as much attention as the Central and Eastern European Countries (CEECs) because they do not really fit into this group. They do not share the same historical and political experiences and above all they are small island states situated "at the other end of Europe" and thus perhaps of rather peripheral importance to the EU. One can conclude that the vast academic contributions dealing with the new members of the fifth enlargement round are inclined to neglect Malta and Cyprus, consequently these two island members are rarely the subject of comprehensive analysis.

In the case of the latter, Cyprus' membership is taken into closer consideration, as the so called "Cyprus question" affects Turkey's efforts for EU-membership.[5]

As far as Malta is concerned, ample sources analysing Malta's path into the EU and what it means for this tiny Mediterranean island to be a member of this "exclusive club" are even harder to find. Malta's size in territorial as well as in political terms and the shift in priorities beginning in the 1990s towards Eastern European countries may have contributed to the lack of these materials.

Already in 1990, Roderick Pace observed:

---

[4] http://europa.eu.int/scadplus/leg/en/lvb/e50017.htm

[5] "Cyprus question" refers to the island's division into a Greek part in the south and a Turkish part since Turkey's occupation of North Cyprus in 1974. For further information on this matter see for example: Redmond (1993a); Redmond (1994).

> "The EC's attention will be turned eastwards for a good number of years to come. Helping the East European economies does not only entail providing them with finance and investments, but also opening the Community's market to them." (Pace 1990, 11)

Pace goes on by stating that

> "(...) their [the Eastern European countries'] political importance will continue to strain the EC's limited resources that can be dished out to its partners. With the ACP countries, the Mediterranean non-member countries and the East Europeans all clamouring for more, the EC will finally share the cake along geopolitical considerations." (Pace 1990, 11)

Thus, a feeling aroused that the Mediterranean applicants and especially Malta may be of secondary importance to the Community.

In contrast to the bulk of academic literature regarding the 2004 EU enlargement round, the focus of this study will be entirely on Malta and her way into the European Union. Special attention will also be given to the positive and negative effects of the accession process on the small island. The aim of this paper is to provide a comprehensive picture of Malta's way into the EU by analysing the island's relationship with the European Union from the very beginning up to now. The underlying perspective will be Malta-EU and not vice versa due to the limited state of research in this field. Furthermore, since national and domestic issues, such as the Maltese political party system, societal factors and foreign policy attitudes will be included in this study, a Malta-EU perspective is certainly more appropriate in this context. At certain points a change in perspective may be required, for example when analysing the European Union's doubts concerning Malta's application for membership, however it will still keep the overall focus in mind.

The basic analytical approach will be political, not economic, which implies that political considerations regarding benefits and disadvantages of close relations with the EU will be in the foreground of the analysis; while economic assessments of pro's and con's for membership will also be touched upon (although not in detail), because they influence and shape the political sphere, and can thus not totally be excluded.

How do factors such as small size, insularity, vulnerability and remoteness influence a small state's behaviour in international relations? What are the major problems and events shaping Malta-EU relations? How can Malta's position in the EU be described? In which way can this small island state defend and enforce its own interests in such a dominant regional organisation in which all members, varying in size and power, try to protect and press ahead their specific aims? This thesis is an attempt to answer these questions and to provide a basis for further discussions and elaboration.

At first, a concise overview of Malta, her geographical position, the historical development as well as the political and economic situation will be presented in order to familiarise the reader with essential key factors.

The following chapter provides the theoretical framework for this study. Major theoretical approaches in fields of Integration theory, foreign policy and small state theory shall be discussed in terms of their applicability for Malta-EU relations. The intention is not to examine every approach in detail, but to outline the main assumptions and to extract some variables and categories which might help explain Malta's position in an international as well as in a regional context.

Subsequently, the development of Malta-EU relations will be discussed in a systematic and analytical manner starting with the island's transformation from a British colony into an independent republic, followed by Malta's first steps towards regional integration, the Association Agreement, the application to join the EU, the suspension of the application and its reactivation, up to Malta becoming a full member of the European Union in 2004. Furthermore, internal problems and debates in society and among political élite concerning membership and its consequences for the small island state will also be included in this analysis. Possible alternatives to EU membership and Malta's representation in EU institutions are further issues which will round off the main part of this study.

The third section will be dedicated to Malta's position within the European Union by analysing the division of power between large and small states in the EU and by looking at selective EU agendas which have particular significance for Malta. Concluding remarks and a concise summary of the findings will complete the study.

2. Malta – Key factors and figures

The Republic of Malta or in Maltese *Repubblika ta' Malta* lies in the heart of the Mediterranean Sea, between Europe and North Africa. The island state is situated 93 km south of Sicily and 288 km north of Tunisia.[6] The country comprises an archipelago – Malta, Gozo and Comino and three much smaller uninhabited islets. The combined area is 316 square kilometres.[7] The island's population amounts to approximately 400,000, making Malta the most densely populated country in Europe, with around 1249 inhabitants per square kilometre. Valletta, the capital, is the cultural, administrative and commercial centre of the archipelago. The official languages are English and Maltese.[8] Catholicism is the predominant religion.

Malta has experienced a turbulent history marked by a number of invasions. The archipelago has been inhabited for some seven thousand years. In the 9th century BC, Phoenician seafarers colonised the Maltese islands. A succession of other rulers followed, notably Carthaginians, Romans, Byzantines and Arabs. In 1530 Malta and Gozo were ceded by the Emperor Charles V to the Order of St. John. After the departure of the Order in 1798, French forces briefly occupied Malta. At the request of the Maltese, the archipelago was placed under British protection in 1799 and formally became part of the British Empire from 1814 under the Treaty of Paris.

Malta gained independence in September 1964 and became a democratic constitutional monarchy.[9] The Constitution was substantially amended on 13 December 1974 turning Malta into an independent parliamentary democracy with a 65 seat unicameral parliament. The 65 members of the House of Representatives (Maltese: *Il-Kamra Tad Deputati*) are elected by a popular vote on the basis of proportional representation, using the single transferable vote

---

6 <http://www.eic.de/fileadmin/user_upload/Malta.pdf>

7 Malta 246 km², Gozo 67 km² and Comino 3 km².

8 Maltese is a language of Semitic origin written in Latin script.

9 Country Profile – Malta (EU document).

method. The President is elected by the House of Representatives for a five-year term, and formally appoints the Prime Minister.[10]

Concerning major economic indicators, Malta's gross domestic product (GDP) per head in power purchasing standards amounted to 69.5% in the year 2001 compared to EU-15, meaning that Malta's GDP was lower than the EU-average, whereas it was much higher in comparison with the average of all new member states (46.6 %). The GDP growth rate in 2002 was 1.7%[11] while the government gross debt in that year was slightly below the EU-15 average.[12] The unemployment rate in 2002 amounted to 6.8 % and was therefore lower than the EU-15 average (7.7 %) and also lower than the average unemployment rate of the new member states (14.8 %).[13]

---

[10] <http://www.mfat.govt.nz/foreign/regions/europe/countrypapers/malta.html>

[11] Year of reference is 1995 (1995 = 100).

[12] Government gross debt as percentage of the GDP; Malta: 61.7 %, EU-15: 62.5% (forecasted)

[13] Figures are taken from: National Statistics Office Malta: Benchmarking Malta in Europe.

3. Theoretical framework

The European Union is an extremely multifaceted organisation. The structure and political system can definitely be described as being *sui generis* in various respects. Its uniqueness is for example reflected in "the way it embodies both supranational and intergovernmental features in its system of governance, and in the extent to which it embodies shared policy responsibilities between different levels of government and different nation states" (Nugent 2003, 465).

Due to this multidimensional nature of the EU, no single theory is able to explain everything. The logic of "deepening and widening the European Union"[14] and the decision-making processes within the EU are such complex matters that more than one conceptual or theoretical tool is needed to analyse and interpret the developments in a satisfactory way.

In many cases, taking into consideration several qualities of theoretical approaches from different schools of thought, might be helpful to handle and conceptualise a given theme.

In this chapter, different approaches from European Integration theory, foreign policy and small state theory will be applied to discuss Malta's position in an international and in a European context as well as in terms of the island's attitudes towards regional integration influenced by changing domestic policies. Not only the range of theories dealing with the European Union, but also the different strands within the above mentioned theories are so great that only the most prominent and most influential approaches can be taken into account.

---

[14] "Deepening" alludes to the ongoing process of political integration by expanding the fields of cooperation as well as EU competencies. "Widening" denotes enlarging the EU by affiliating new member states.

3.1 Theories of European Integration

Innumerable works theorising economic and political integration in Europe have been published over the past decades.

> "Many scholars of European integration have explored ways in which the overall nature of the integration process might be theorised. The purpose of such exploration has been to develop a broad understanding of the factors underlying European integration and in so doing to facilitate predictions of how integration is likely to proceed". (Nugent 2003, 478-479)

Two influential and ground-breaking approaches of integration theory are neo-functionalism and liberal intergovernmentalism.

Neo-functionalism, dating back to the 1950s and 1960s is based mainly on David Mitrany's functionalist approach and can be classified as a traditional theory of European integration. Its major advocates are Ernst B. Haas and Leon N. Lindberg. Neo-functionalism aims to shed light on the inner dynamics of the integration process.[15] The central idea of neo-functionalism is the "spill-over" concept. According to Lindberg, "spill-over refers to a situation in which a given action, related to a specific goal, creates a situation in which the original goal can be assured only by taking further actions, which in turn create a further condition and a need for more action, and so forth". (Lindberg 1963, 10). In other words, neo-functionalists assume that integration between states in one particular field will quickly create strong incentives for further integration in other fields in order to fully benefit from the original cooperation in the first field. Neo-functionalists argue that supranational institutions of the European Union are the central actors and thus the driving forces in the European integration process. The difference and possibly the strength of the neo-functionalist approach is, in contrast to other theories, that it was specifically modelled on European integration by trying to explain the integration process on the basis of empirical data and that unlike previous approaches, it tends to be more descriptive than normative. During the 1960s and 1970s, neo-functionalism lost much of its explanatory power, because its depiction of

[15] See also Tömmel (2005), p. 5.

the integration process did not provide any explanations for phases of stagnation or setbacks.[16]

> "The slowing down of the integration process following the 1965-6 crisis in the EC and the world economic recession of the early 1970s was thus something of a jolt for advocates of neofunctionalism". (Nugent 2003, 480)

Haas himself later acknowledged the insufficiencies of the neo-functionalist approach and retreated from it. However, in the late 1980s, due to the revitalisation of the integration process, neo-functionalism saw a partial comeback. Even today, the unquestionable eligibility and significance of the neo-functionalist approach justifies its key-position in the field of integration theory.

In political science, neo-functionalism is often contrasted with intergovernmentalism, an influential theory, developed in the 1990s, with roots in the realist tradition. In simplified terms, the basic assumption of realism is that nation states are the main actors in international affairs and that, unlike neo-functionalism, supranational or non-governmental actors within a state are of minor importance.[17] Robert O. Keohane and Stanley Hoffmann proposed an alternative realist approach by depicting European integration as "a strategy consciously adopted by states within the European institutions, to achieve their interest" (Pace 2001, 83).

This line of thinking led to the emergence of the so called liberal intergovernmentalism represented by its foremost proponent Andrew Moravcsik. Liberal intergovernmentalism attempts to analyse the functioning of international organisations with special reference to the question to which degree and under which circumstances cooperation between states takes place. The underlying assumption is that states act according to rational state behaviour, meaning they tend to utilise the most appropriate method to achieve their goals and

---

[16] Particularly, Charles de Gaulle's "empty chair" politics triggered a blockade in political integration at that time.

[17] Nugent (2003), 482.

specific interests in the international arena. As Ingeborg Tömmel points out states are willing to cooperate if they anticipate advantages for themselves:

> „Im Rahmen des Intergouvernementalismus wird die zwischenstaatliche Kooperation aus der Perspektive der nutzenmaximierenden, interessengeleiteten und rational handelnden staatlichen Akteuren erklärt. So kann zwischenstaatliche Kooperation (...) zu Stande kommen, wenn die Erzielung besserer Resultate beziehungsweise konkreter Vorteile (im Vergleich zur Nicht-Kooperation) zu erwarten ist; weitere Motive können die Möglichkeiten zu Tauschgeschäften zwischen den Kooperationspartnern oder auch nur die Angst vor Nachteilen im Falle des drohenden Ausschlusses von der Kooperation sein". (Tömmel 2005, 4)

Besides rational state behaviour, national preference formation and interstate bargaining are the fundamental components of liberal intergovernmentalism. National preference formation refers to national governments and societal factors, meaning governments respond to changing domestic pressures and interactions, which in turn are often closely linked to economic interdependence. Following national preference formation, interstate bargaining comes into play. Interstate bargaining denotes an intergovernmentalist interpretation of interstate relations which considers the relative bargaining powers of a government in inter-state negotiations as a decisive factor concerning the outcome of the negotiation. Thus, the aspired policy-coordination is determined by strategic interaction between the states.[18]

Later, Moravcsik added a third stage of decision-making, namely institutional choice. The main concern in this stage is to clarify why states choose to delegate or pool decision-making in international institutions.[19] In this respect, the European Union clearly differs from other international organisations because of the pooling of sovereignty through qualified majority voting and the delegation of sovereign powers to semi-autonomous institutions such as the European Court of Justice (ECJ) and the Commission.[20]

---

[18] Compare also Nugent (2003), 482; Laursen [n.d.], 12.

[19] Each of the three stages (national preference formation, interstate bargaining and institutional choice) is explained by a different theory, which will not be described in detail here.

[20] See also Laursen [n.d.], 13; Pace (2001), 87.

Despite its structured and plausible composition and its proven ability to explain parts of the European integration process, especially in connection with the Single European Act (SEA), liberal intergovernmentalism has mainly been criticised for understating the influence of supranational institutions such as the Commission and the ECJ as well as transnational actors, for example globally operating companies and influential interest groups.[21]

A third conceptualisation of European integration, which recently attracted attention in European circles is the multi-level governance approach introduced by Gary Marks and Lisbet Hooghe.[22] Multi-level governance rejects the state-centric model of intergovernmentalism by stating that power and influence are exercised at multiple levels of government, e.g. on a supranational, national, regional and local level. The multi-level governance approach is very useful in explaining the interaction of the above mentioned levels of government, but it still has to be developed into a fully-fledged theory of European integration and will thus not be part of deeper analysis in this study.[23]

After having outlined the major assumptions of the most influential European integration theories, the question remains to which extent are they capable to elucidate Malta's status in a regional and international context as well as her role in the European integration process.

Both neo-functionalism and liberal intergovernmentalism provide only basic interpretations concerning European Union enlargement. Nevertheless, conclusions regarding the EU enlargement round in 2004 can be drawn from the general conception of both theories and their respective premises.[24]

Barbara Lippert states that neo-functionalism regards the Eastern Enlargement of the European Union as a kind of "geographical spill-over" which strengthens the political and economic cohesion of the Community. More-

---

[21] Cf. Nugent (2003), 483.

[22] For a detailed analysis of this approach see Marks/ Hooghe (2004).

[23] For further criticism concerning the multi-level governance approach see also Knodt/ Große Hüttmann (2005).

[24] See also the schema developed by Barbara Lippert concerning EU-enlargement and integration theories in Lippert (2004), 16f.

over, the outstanding role of the Commission during the complex negotiation process is emphasised as well as the relationship of tension between deepening and widening the EU:

> „Der Ansatz [neofunctionalism] bezieht sich vor allem auf das Verhalten von Gemeinschaftsakteuren, insbesondere die Rolle der Kommission als Motor der Erweiterungspolitik, (...). Danach sind die Verhandlungsergebnisse mehr als die Summe der Einzelinteressen der Mitgliedstaaten. Problematisiert wird auch das Spannungsverhältnis zwischen Erweiterung und Vertiefung, wobei der Bewahrung und Fortentwicklung des Acquis im Zuge der Erweiterung besondere Bedeutung zukommt.“ (Lippert 2004, 19)

From this point of view, the enlargement of the EU including the two Mediterranean islands Cyprus and Malta can be regarded as a consistent step of EU expansion, i.e. that the geographical spill-over is not exclusively directed towards the east but also south to the coast of North Africa.

As far as liberal intergovernmentalism is concerned, Lippert points out the bargaining processes at the enlargement summits, which may lead to detailed transitional agreements, are best explained with the help of the intergovernmentalist approach.[25] Furthermore, in this context enlargement is closely linked to national preferences formation of single states:

> "Die Erweiterung bietet der Union aus Sicht des liberalen Intergouvernementalismus insgesamt die Chance, die neuen wirtschaftlichen und sozialen Interdependenzen vom Handel bis hin zur Migration besser zu managen. Als rationale Akteure haben die Mitgliedstaaten jedoch ihre 'nationalen Interessen' fest im Blick und kalkulieren die potenziellen Chancen und die Kosten des Beitritts neuer Mitglieder." (Lippert 2004, 19)

But how does the intergovernmentalist approach judge the balance of powers once the new members, and as in the case of Cyprus and Malta small states, have joined the Community?

Here Roderick Pace makes clear that

> "according to the Liberal-Intergovernmentalist approach, from its inception the EC has always been an intergovernmental organisation based on bargaining between the member states. The larger ones exercise a *de facto*

[25] Lippert (2004), 18.

> veto, while the smaller ones can be bought off with side payments in order to facilitate agreement. Member states can also be impelled to accept an outcome by threat of exclusion." (Pace 2001, 85)

To sum up, it can be stated that European Integration theory provides basic and useful concepts for the enlargement process in general and the perception of power balances within the EU. However, to extract detailed theoretical assumptions concerning the specific area of Malta-EU relations would mean to overstretch the explanatory power of neo-functionalism and liberal intergovernmentalism. Thus, further approaches from other schools of thought need to be taken into account in order to detect categories or variables which might specify Malta's position in a world context.

3.2. Foreign Policy Approaches

International relations theory offers a wide range of perspectives from which relations between states can be analysed and conceptualised. As shown in the previous subchapter, one way is to analyse the processes leading to cooperation between states and the development of integration. Another method is to confine the perspective to the foreign policy behaviour of particular states. These foreign policy approaches, as derivatives of international relations theory, share basic assumptions with realist and liberal paradigms, which means that overlaps between the different branches of international relation theory do occur.

The foreign policy approaches which will be discussed here in order to locate variables which may help to interpret Malta's position in international relations are neorealism, utilitarian liberalism and constructivism.

3.2.1 Neorealism

Neorealism, also often termed "structural realism", is centred around different fundamental assumptions concerning states and the international system. Kenneth Waltz, a leading advocate of neorealism, specifies these assumptions in his book *Theory of International Politics*. The first assumption is that rationally acting states are the main actors in the international arena. According to neorealism, the international system itself is anarchic and marked by changing power structures.[26] Such an anarchic world system creates a general sense of insecurity, which often results in what neorealists call a "security dilemma". States seek to handle this ubiquitous dilemma by self-help:

> "Since there is no "world state" to protect the fundamental interests of the individual political communities, states are bound to secure their survival and welfare ultimately through self-help." (Rittberger 2005, 3f.)

Based on these assumptions, major components of foreign policy behaviour can be deduced. These are the striving for security and power. Closely coupled to security and power are the state's fundamental interests to preserve or extend its autonomy and influence.[27]

Power in this sense is primarily defined as military and economic capability as well as in terms of territory and population. "The more powerful a state, the more autonomy for itself and the more influence over other states or collective decision-making it strives for" (Baumann et al. 2000, 2). Concerning the concepts of autonomy and influence in foreign policy behaviour, these can best be explained by looking at specific examples. A foreign policy based on autonomy serves to preserve and increase autonomy, whereas a foreign policy which is slanted towards influence secures and extends its influence over other states and within international institutions.[28]

In general, autonomy and influence are related in a way that gaining in one field entails a loss in the other. But in case of strengthening supranational institutions, like the European Union, by extending their responsibilities, there is a considerable loss of autonomy without a gain in influence for the state. Only the supranational institution, e.g. the EU, gains autonomy.[29]

---

[26] See also Rittberger/ Andrei (2005), 32.

[27] Cf. Baumann et al. (2000), 4.

[28] Baumann et al. (2000), 10.

[29] Cf. Baumann et al. (2000), 12.

The conclusion which can be drawn from this example is that from a neo-realist point of view state cooperation and the integration of states in supra-national organisations are regarded as being rather destructive, because the expected profit for the single state, e.g. the augmentation of influence and power, is fairly minimal.

If one goes one step further and looks at the foreign policy behaviour of a great power, such as the United States of America, in comparison to the foreign policy behaviour of a small state, it can be stated that a small state, like Malta, seems to be too weak to pursue a successful policy based on influence or autonomy at all. "Its interest in autonomy and influence is by no means less than that of a great power, but its opportunities for actually pursuing autonomy- and influence-seeking policy are far fewer" (Baumann et al, 10).

3.2.2. Utilitarian Liberalism

Like neorealism, utilitarian liberalism works from the assumption that actors are self-interested and rationally pursue mainly materialistic goals. The underlying model of both approaches is the so called *homo oeconomicus*. According to the *homo oeconomicus* model, besides self-interest and rationality, "actors consciously pursue goals which they strive to attain at minimum costs. From among the choices facing them, these actors pick the one that is optimal given their preferences and the constraints they face" (Rittberger 2005, 8).

A major difference between neorealism and utilitarian liberalism is that for utilitarian liberalists the main political actors are individuals and groups, e.g. political and administrative actors, companies, economic pressure groups, social and political advocacy groups[30], whereas neorealists perceive unitary states as the key actors. Resulting from these different perceptions, in utilitarian liberalist terms, not international constraints (anarchic system, security dilemma, changing power structures) but domestic interest determine a state's

---

[30] See also schema provided by Bienen et al. (2000), 18f.

foreign policy behaviour.[31] To secure one's own (social) survival must be regarded as the essential interest of any actor or group, because only then the pursuit of other utility-increasing aims is possible.[32]

Thus, the societal actor's basic motivation is gain-seeking in order to increase utility. Gain, in this context, can be either material, e.g. assets or income, or immaterial, for example competencies.[33]

In order to explain foreign policy behaviour in detail from a utilitarian liberalist point of view, the policy network approach is used to identify those societal actors whose interests are most likely to influence the foreign policy of the country.[34]

After having outlined the mode of action and the fundamental assumptions of utilitarian liberalism, it should have become clear that this approach is rather inapplicable to explain Malta's position in an *international* context, because the focus of utilitarian liberalism is more on the domestic factors and on the specific interests of societal actors. Nevertheless, it is a valuable contribution regarding the analysis of the influence of political and administrative actors as well as different social groups on a state's foreign policy behaviour.

Such pressures which societal actors are able to exercise will be the subject of further analysis later in this study, when Malta's changing attitudes towards the European Union are taken into consideration.

3.2.3. Constructivism

A third influential theory in the field of foreign policy, though not completely inconsistent with the neorealist and liberalist paradigms, is the so called con-

---

[31] Compare also Bienen et al. (2000), 2.

[32] See also Bienen et al. (2000), 5.

[33] Cf. Rittberger (2005), 16.

[34] Rittberger (2005), 28. Such a detailed identification of every actor's interests cannot be discussed here, due to the limited scope of this paper. For further information on this subject, see Rittberger/ Andrei (2005), 37ff.

structivist approach. The founder of constructivism, the American political scientist Alexander Wendt, explains his concept as follows:

> "My objective (...) is to build a bridge between these two traditions [neorealism and neoliberalism] (...) by developing a constructivist argument, drawn from structurationist and symbolic interactionist sociology, on behalf of the liberal claim that international institutions can transform state identities and interests. In contrast to the 'economic' theorizing that dominates mainstream systemic international scholarship, this involves a 'sociological social psychological' form of systemic theory in which identities and interests are the dependent variable." (Wendt 1992, 394)

In constructivism, the model of the *homo oeconomicus*[35] is replaced by the model of a *homo sociologicus* or "role player":

> "In contrast to *homo oeconomicus, homo sociologicus* is not 'programmed' by a given set of goals that preordain certain actions. Rather the actor plays a social role (or rather several roles) which he has acquired through a process of socialization (...)". (Rittberger 2005, 8f.)

Thus, constructivists, for example, look at threats, fears and identities as the social constructs of the actors. Another essential assumption of constructivism is that there is no "logic" of anarchy in the international system, but "anarchy is what states make of it" (Wendt 1992, 395).

Following these assumptions, a constructivist foreign policy behaviour is not based on power or gains as in neorealism and utilitarian liberalism, but on norms. In this context, norms are defined as "value-based, shared expectations about appropriate behavior" and as such, norms "shape actors' identities and preferences, define collective goals and prescribe or proscribe behavior".[36] As a consequence, actors proceed according to social norms and their social role. Concerning foreign policy behaviour, decision-makers are at the same time subject to international as well as societal socialisation processses.

To which extent a norm influences foreign policy behaviour depends on two variables, namely *commonality* and *specificity*. The commonality of a norm re-

---

[35] See also page 16 in this study.

[36] Boekle et al. (2000), 3.

fers to the number of actors of one social system sharing value-based expectations of behaviour whereas specificity denotes to which degree a norm distinguishes appropriate from inappropriate behaviour.[37]

Such a detailed constructivist perspective of foreign policy behaviour is apparently not free from criticism. First of all, actors are "frequently confronted with many value-based expectations of behavior, with the result that a distinction between relevant and irrelevant expectations of behavior is made difficult or becomes arbitrary" (Boekle et al. 2000, 7). As a consequence, constructivism runs the risk to "explain" a given foreign policy behaviour in retrospect by choosing a specific explanation which best describes the expected behaviour.[38]

Another point of criticism even more relevant in the context of this study is that constructivism does not offer criteria for determining whether foreign policy actors are primarily influenced by international norms or their societal environment.

> "If there are conflicting societal and international norms, a constructivist explanation is indeterminate because in such situations, foreign policy decision-makers are free to choose the norm which best justifies their behavior." (Boekle et al. 2000, 11)

Due to this danger of retrospectively explaining social behaviour and the fact that the expectations of behaviour addressed by international institutions or by domestic society cannot clearly be separated, constructivism, for the purpose of circumscribing Malta's status in international relations, seems to be rather unsuitable. Since, especially in the case of Malta, the separation of expected behaviour from an international and a domestic or societal context is of major importance in analysing the island's status in the world.

The overall conclusions which can be drawn from this concise analysis of foreign policy approaches is that neorealism considers small states as being incapable to pursue an effective foreign policy based on power, influence and

---

[37] Boekle et al. (2000), 7.

[38] Boekle et al. (2000), 7.

autonomy. Neither do neorealists see a real advantage for small states if they build alliances with more powerful nations as means to overcome this difficulty. The contribution of utilitarian liberalism to this study is that it offers an approach to analyse to which extent domestic social pressures influence the foreign policy behaviour of Malta. Constructivism as the third leading foreign policy approach, in my estimation, does not offer apt categories for the analysis of Malta's foreign policy behaviour and will therefore be neglected in the in the course of this paper.

3.3. Small State Theory

A third and last element of international relations theory which will be taken into account in order to provide a coherent theoretical framework for this study is small state theory. Small state theory is not as well established as the above mentioned theories which contributes to the fact that this approach is often neglected by political scientists:

> "(...) the realist paradigm dominant in the study of international relations posits that the 'big players' are worthy of the most scholarly attention because they are the shapers of the international system (Waltz 1979) – which essentially relegates research on small states to a subordinate status within political science." (Hey 2003, 5)

Nevertheless, small state theory enriches international relations theory and it provides a very useful theoretical tool for analysing the small island of Malta and her position in an international context.

Consequently, the focus of this subchapter will be on the role of small states – such as Malta – their behaviour and the problems they might face in the international system as well as the competitive advantages they may have compared to larger countries. Small state theory also deals with foreign policy behaviour, however from a different angle than outlined in the previous subchapter about universal foreign policy approaches. In small state theory the main concern is on small states' foreign policy behaviour and on the question whether it is possible to compare foreign policy attitudes of small states and to detect common behavioural patterns. Regional integration is certainly one topic, which will be touched upon in this context, but from a more general point of view, because the debate concerning small states within the European Union, as one body of regional integration, will be a matter of detailed analysis later on.[39]

From today's point of view, Wilhelm Christmas-Møller illustrates the peculiarities of the small state approach as follows:

> "Few concepts within political science have been attacked as fiercely as the concept of small state and have still been used for political analysis. In this respect the concept resembles the real world to which it refers. Several times in modern history, the ruin and extinction of small states has been predicted. In spite of these gloomy predictions both concept and its counterpart in the real world have demonstrated a surprising ability to survive all threats and difficulties.".(Christmas-Møller 1983, 35)

After the Second World War, research on small states slowly developed. Annette Baker Fox's book *The Power of Small States* [40], in the style of the American realist school, is generally seen as the cornerstone of small state theory, although European studies in this field did exist before, though unfortunately, never reached the same appreciation.[41] However the height of small state research in Europe, partly influenced by behaviourism, can be found in the beginning of the 1970s up to the beginning of the 1980s, coinciding with an economic revival.[42] Later on in the 1980s, small state research was confronted with a phase of stagnation:

> "It is interesting to observe and to denote that in spite of the increasing importance of the political phenomenon of small states in Europe (...) small state research in Europe is not taking up the clues and the methodological and theoretical findings and achievements of the Critical European school of small state theorizing in the 70ies and the early 80ies, but is rather 'developing back' to the limited traditional vista of security and dependency dilemmas of big power analysis". (Höll/ Kramer, cited in Koßdorff 2000, 16)

---

[39] Cf. 7.1. Large States versus Small States in an enlarged Union?

[40] Baker Fox (1959).

[41] Cf. Christmas-Møller (1983), 36.

[42] See also Kramer (1983), 251 ff.

With the collapse of the Soviet Union, a number of small states have entered the world scene, which at the same time has led to a revaluation of small state theory.[43] In general, it should be noted that today's small state theory does not constitute one uniform approach, but rather a discipline with a rich choice of different theoretical and methodological approaches, none of which is predominant.[44]

The criticism of the small state approach has mainly evolved around three crucial points, i.e. defining "smallness", the problems of small states and their behaviour and strategies.

3.3.1. Difficulties in defining "smallness"

A major problem and one of the major causes for disputes among scholars in the field of small state theory is to find and agree on a convincing and reliable classification of smallness:

> "Nobody doubted the existence of small states, most scholars also seemed to have a rather clear idea of what might be considered typical properties, but the problem was to identify the phenomenon as a separate category distinct from neighbouring categories, because the social world is not organized in distinct groups but on a continuum with transition from one category to the next." (Christmas-Møller 1983, 40)

States can be categorised according to different variables. The most common ones are territory, population, GDP, power and military or economic capacities. Several variables can also be combined for reasons of classification. According to these criteria, states can be described as "large", "medium" "small", "micro" or "mini" states, while "small" is often automatically equated with "weak" or "dependent" state. It needs to be clarified that it might be true that a small state is at the same time a weak state, but not automatically and thus "small" and "weak" should not be used synonymously in this context.[45]

---

[43] Before 1989 small states in Europe constituted a proportion of 69,7%, after 1993 the statistical dominance of small states amounted to 82,2% (cf. Koßdorff 2000, 14).

[44] Cf. Höll (1983), 15.

[45] See also Koßdorff (2000), 35.

As far as population is concerned, Goldhamer pinpoints the problem of definition in an exaggerated, but striking way:

> "The term 'small country' seems to be reserved for large countries with small populations, small countries with large populations, small countries with small populations, and sometimes countries of any size that mostly mind their own business in world affairs." (Goldhamer, cited in Koßdorff 2000, 29)

Attempts to rank small states vary from 7,000 to 15 million inhabitants.[46] In social sciences, a computer based, so called "cluster analysis" is applied to classify states according to the categories of population, size and GDP. With the help of this analysis, about 45 "micro" states of smallest size could be identified, among them Malta and Cyprus.[47] Such classifications have been criticised by various authors, for example Hans A. Mouritzen's states that "(...) the main difficulty is, of course, that any division of the size variable into separate categories is arbitrary (...). There are no qualitative divisions in reality that justify a particular size categorization; this is so whether we use area, population or GNP as our criterion of division" (Mouritzen, 239-240).[48]

The American political scientist Robert O. Keohane suggests a different approach of classification, namely according to a state's systemic role in international politics. He distinguishes between four different systemic roles: *System-determining* states play a decisive role and may change the political system, *system-influencing* states can influence the system's nature through unilateral or multilateral action, *system-affecting* states are not able to influence the system alone, but in cooperation with others and *system-ineffectual* states are those states which are not able to influence the system, they rather adjust to reality than actively shaping it.[49]

---

[46] Pace (2001), 15.

[47] Cf. Waschkuhn (1993), 10f. for a list of all 45 states belonging to this group. For information about Malta's population, size and GDP see: 2. Malta – Key factors and figures in this study.

[48] Harvey Armstrong and Robert Read argue in the same vein; Armstrong/ Read (1995), 1230.

[49] Cf. Pace (2001), 18; Koßdorff (2000), 35.

Hans Geser offers a third concept of smallness, namely that a state can be classified as small, if the state *perceives* itself as small and if also other states confirm such a *perception*. Geser calls this type of smallness "perceived" or "attributive" smallness.[50] For example, Jeanne A.K. Hey employs this concept of smallness in her book *Small States in World Politics: Explaining Foreign Policy Behaviour*.[51]

The question remains, which conclusions can be drawn for Malta concerning these discussions about defining smallness? First of all, it is rather indisputable that Malta with a population slightly below 400,000 and a territory of 316 square kilometres *perceives* herself as "small" and that neighbouring countries and the European Union have the same attitude, e.g. since Malta's accession in 2004, Malta is often correctly described as the smallest member state of the European Union (in terms of territory and population).

Secondly, according to Keohane's systemic schema, it seems to be most suitable to classify Malta as a *system-ineffectual* state, e.g. a state that rather adjusts to the international system than actively shaping it. However, Roderick Pace's assumption that through EU membership and participation in decision-making institutions of the Union, Malta possibly transforms from a *system-ineffectual* to a *system-affecting* state still needs to be verified in the course of the paper.[52]

Thirdly, although several authors suggest to classify Malta as a "micro state",[53] in this study the Mediterranean island state will be grouped into the broader category of "small states", because I share Mouritzen's opinion that any clear demarcation according to size is rather arbitrary and not very useful for analytical purposes. Furthermore, I do not regard a subdivision in "small" and smallest states or "micro states" as meaningful, because I assume that the problems as well as advantages small states and so called "micro-states"

---

[50] Cf. Geser (2001), 89f.

[51] Cf. Hey (2003), 3.

[52] Cf. Pace (2001), 50.

[53] Cf. Pace (2001) or the cluster analysis implemented by Sieglinde Gstöhl, cited in Waschkuhn (1993), 11.

have, are very much the same and consequently there is no need to make use of further categorisations.

3.3.2. Problems and strategies of small states

In contrast to the manifold opinions regarding the definition of smallness, there exists substantial consensus between scholars of small state research about the *problems* of small states in the international system. In general, small states' difficulties can be identified in two major spheres. The first one is the political, the other, the economic sphere.

The prevailing problematic area in the political sphere of small states is security, or more precisely, "the ability of a state to avoid or overcome any violent threat to its territorial integrity, politico-economic independence or institutional arrangements".[54] As Vandenbosch points out: "A small state (...) is a state which is *unable to contend in war with great powers* on anything like equal terms" (Vandenbosch, cited in Koßdorff 2000, 41). An important term in this context is vulnerability. One aspect of vulnerability refers to the condition that small states are mostly unable to provide for their own security and are therefore easily exposed to threats from larger countries.[55]

The question which has to be posed is: What options do small states have to overcome or at least diminish this vulnerability and to protect themselves? Three main strategies frequently suggested and often adopted by small states are to form alliances, to proclaim neutrality or to apply for membership in international organisations.

Different types of alliances are conceivable. An alliance between small states is one example, but this kind of alliance is often regarded as not being very beneficial due to the lack of influence and power. Another type is a bilateral alliance between a small state and a more powerful state. The bigger power guarantees the weaker or more vulnerable state (military) support in case of

---

[54] Espíndola (1987), 64.

[55] Vulnerability also plays a vital role in the economic sphere and the term is also used in connection with proneness to natural disasters. These issues will be picked up later on.

an outside aggression. Though helpful, alliances of this kind are not totally unproblematic. For Rothstein the greatest danger is that the small state may become a satellite of the bigger state.[56] Thus, Rothstein sees multilateral alliances between small and big states as the best option for a small state: "Small Powers *ought* to prefer mixed, multilateral alliances. They provide the most benefits in terms of security and political influence" (Rothstein, cited in Koßdorff 2000, 43). As will be shown in detail later on, Malta made extensive use of this strategy of varying alliances under the political leadership of Dom Mintoff, but only with moderate success.

Alliances in general have lost some of their attraction, because the number of acute military threats have declined during the last decades. Nowadays, due to growing interdependence, survival of small states is no longer restricted to a narrow military sense, but comprises several fields.[57]

Neutrality is often seen as an adequate alternative to alliances. Newly independent states which belonged for a long time to a colonial power were inclined to use this strategy in world affairs to assert their formal independence.[58] Neutrality means not taking sides in a war between other parties and in return not being attacked by the conflicting parties. Non-alignment is also often subsumed under the concept of neutrality, although non-alignment goes beyond the case of war, because non-alignment denotes the wilful desistence from military alliances to preserve neutrality in case of an armed conflict with the underlying aim to prevent a war altogether. During the Cold War, an international organisation named Non-Aligned Movement (NAM) was established. The members of NAM consider themselves as not formally aligned with or against any major power bloc. The concept of neutrality and also the Non-Aligned Movement has lost much of its significance since the end of the Cold War:

> "As traditionally conceptualised, neutrality has been found to be largely irrelevant in the post-cold war era, unable to contend with the highly interde-

[56] Rothstein (1968); cited in Pace (2001), 25.

[57] For a more detailed analysis concerning alliances see Reiter/ Gärtner (2001).

[58] See also Pace (2001), 26f.

> pendent nature of the contemporary international system and the diffuse nature of the threats it harbours." (Bauwens et al. 1996; cited in Pace 2001, 28)[59]

Malta was a member of NAM before joining the European Union. Furthermore, the Republic of Malta has codified neutrality, or more specifically non-alignment, in its constitution in chapter 1, article 1(3):

> "Malta is a neutral state actively pursuing peace, security and social progress among all nations by adhering to a policy of non-alignment and refusing to participate in any military alliance".[60]

The island's neutral position led to some controversial discussions in Malta-EU relations.[61]

Besides alliances and neutrality, membership in international organisations is another useful strategy for small states to enhance their security. "As the world has become increasingly more integrated and the number of issues to be dealt with in the international arena has grown, the need for small states to integrate with their neighbours has grown as well".[62]

Or as Roderick Pace points out in an article in the *South European Society & Politics* journal:

> "Small states' interests are often better served by the international rule of law than by an anarchical international system based on the struggle for power. Hence they tend to exhibit a preference for international organizations and rule-based regimes."[63]

For a small state, being part of an international organisation, for example the United Nations, means being on equal footing with larger countries and to have the opportunity to make oneself heard. Furthermore, due to their military

---

[59] Bauwens,/ Clesse/ Knudsen (1996).

[60] Constitution of Malta http://docs.justice.gov.mt/lom/legislation/english/leg/vol_1/chapt0.pdf.

[61] The issue of Malta's neutrality will be taken up again under 4.3. and 4.4. in this study.

[62] Bayar (2003), 27.

[63] Pace (2002), cited in Walker/ Elliott (2004), 173.

weakness, small states normally do not act as aggressors in international politics, but they take over the function of mediators or peace-keepers:

> "Small powers frequently offer mediation or peace-keeping services in conflict situations because of their lack in direct involvement in crisis areas. Their lower status and level of international involvement may allow them to undertake certain tasks that would be denied by the contestants to major powers." (Holsti, cited in Koßdorff 2000, 44) [64]

Malta joined the United Nations in 1964 and one year later the small island also became a member of the Council of Europe.

It still needs to be analysed if membership in the European Union, as a specific type of an international organisation, is also an appropriate means to diminish a small state's vulnerability.

As already mentioned above small states do not only have to face problems in the political sphere, but they are also vulnerable in economic terms. Some scholars even state that nowadays economic dependence is a more severe problem than the question of security:

> "Small states (besides their security problem) also have a problem of survival in their trade policy, which under most circumstances and during the longest periods seems far more important than their security problem." (Pedersen, cited in Koßdorff 2000, 47)

Paul Streeten identifies the following economic disadvantages of small states in comparison to larger states: a less diversified economic structure, limited raw materials and natural resources, a small domestic market causing a limited ability to exploit economies of scale and heavy dependence on foreign trade.[65] Moreover, a lack of qualified human resources may also be a problem for small economies.[66] Shmuel Noah Eisenstadt sees "specialization for special external markets, stemming from either the geographical location or

---

[64] Holsti (1970).

[65] Streeten (1993), 197f. Cf. Briguglio (1995), 1616.

[66] See also Abt/ Deutsch (1993) 21.

the specific features of social and economic structure and cultural traditions" as one compensating measure for small state economies.[67]

In small state research only few advantages arising from smallness have been identified and these are regarded as being outweighed by the disadvantages:

> "The few advantages derived from small size identified in the micro-state literature are generally intangible and therefore impossible to quantify. For example, it has been frequently asserted that micro-states have greater social homogeneity and cohesion, greater social flexibility and openness to change (...). These attributes facilitate greater single-mindedness and focus in economic policy making and a more rapid and effective response to exogenous change." (Armstrong/ Read 1995, 1230)

Is smallness thus inherently a disadvantageous factor in economic terms? For Khalaf, who conducted a study in which he compared specific economic data of 80 countries with varying sizes, it is not:

> "Size does not have any clear impact on economic stability nor on economic growth and development. 'Smallness' is not a source of extra instability, nor is smallness necessarily an obstacle to economic growth and development." (Khalaf, cited in Koßdorff 2000, 48)[68]

Positive economic developments of small states such as Austria, Switzerland or Denmark also seem to underline that theory is not always congruent with practice. It will be shown later on in this study that economic and respectively financial considerations played a vital role in Malta-EU relations.

3.3.3. Small states' foreign policy behaviour

A third and last point which has to be discussed in connection with small state theory is the small states' attitudes in foreign policy. Is it possible to identify a common foreign policy behaviour of small states? Which strategies do small states utilise in order to gain recognition in the international system?

---

[67] Eisenstadt (1993), 110.

[68] Khalaf (1971); see also Borda (1997).

A state's priorities in foreign policy are closely connected to its geographic position, its history and its economy.[69] A factor which logically limits a state's foreign policy activities are the state's resources (personnel, money, influence) as Thomas Jansen points out:

> "Es ist evident, daß die Außenpolitik eines Staates nur so weit reicht wie seine Mittel reichen – und die Mittel eines kleinen Staates reichen in der Regel nicht, um eine weltumspannende Außenpolitik zu betreiben." (Jansen 2001, 171)

The most common strategies or behaviours employed or at least expected to be used by small states in foreign policy are a low level of participation in world affairs, addressing a narrow scope of foreign policy issues, focusing on neighbouring geographic areas, employing diplomatic and economic foreign policy instruments instead of military instruments and joining international institutions.[70] The assumption, developed during the height of small states research in the 1960s and 1970s, that due to their comparability in size, small states also pursue a similar foreign policy is nowadays no longer tenable.[71] Small states have several strategies at their disposal and they use them according to their specific situation.

Another aspect is the separation of foreign and domestic policy. Especially in the realist tradition it is argued that both policies have to be clearly separated. Nevertheless, in the case of Malta there is definitely a close connection between domestic decision-making and foreign policy behaviour or in other words, in Malta "foreign policy has always acted as the hand-maiden of domestic policy".[72]

Malta is also a special case in another respect. Malta is not only a small state, but it is a small *island* state. The issue of insularity should not be underestimated in small state research. Prof. Lino Briguglio, director of the *Islands*

---

[69] Cf. Jansen (2001), 170.

[70] Cf. Hey (2003), 5; Pace (2001), 5 or with a slightly different notion Koßdorff (2000), 56-57.

[71] Cf. Gstöhl (2001), 103; Christmas-Møller (1983), 46.

[72] Pace (2001), 5.

& Small States Institute in Malta, conducted a study on behalf of the United Nations Conference on Trade and Development (UNCTAD) on small island developing states and their economic vulnerabilities and disadvantages.[73] Besides the already mentioned disadvantages of small states, he identified remoteness and proneness to natural disasters as special vulnerabilities. Insularity and remoteness may lead to high per-unit transport costs, uncertainties of supply and additional costs for warehouses to keep large stocks.[74]

To finalise the discussion about small state theory it should be kept in mind that

> "smallness is neither intrinsically ugly nor beautiful. It simply represents an additional set of factors which have to be considered. By skilful political leadership and a policy of diversifying dependency, states can take advantage of its positive aspects and minimize its disadvantages. How they actually do so will vary from case to case according to multiple other factors more important than the fact of smallness." (Clarke/ Payne 1987, 228)

[73] See Bhuglah et al. [n.d.].

[74] Briguglio (1995), 1615ff.; Borg (1993), 71.

4. Development of Malta-EU relations

After having established a differentiated and firm theoretical framework for the following analysis, the development of Malta-EU relations can now be taken into detailed consideration. This shall be done in a historical-analytical way by not only outlining and examining major steps in Malta-EU relations, but also by shedding light on the (internal) conflicts and forces behind this development. For example, references to the particularities of the Maltese party system or Malta's contacts with neighbouring countries in the Mediterranean basin will serve to better understand the whole process, and help provide a comprehensive and multi-faceted picture of Malta's way into the European Union.

4.1. After Malta's Independence: orientation and deterioration

On September 21st 1964, after 150 years of British rule, Malta formally gained independence from the United Kingdom. These long years under foreign ruling posed a serious problem for the Maltese government, namely how to manage the island's transition from a British military base, in which defence spending served as reliable economic pillar, into a viable economic unit.[75] In order to mitigate a sudden economic shock, the Prime Minister at that time, Giorgio Borg Olivier from the Nationalist Party, negotiated a Defence and Financial Agreement with Britain.[76] The agreement was designed to facilitate economic development. It was agreed that Britain would provide £51 million in loans and grants over a ten-year period for Malta.

Nevertheless, the Maltese government knew that the agreement could only be a short-term solution, since the gradual retreat of British military presence

[75] Cf. Craig (1987), 170.

[76] Borg Olivier was Prime Minister from 1950 to 1955 and from 1962 to 1971. The Nationalist Party and its policies will be subject of closer analysis under 4.2. Malta's political culture and party system.

entailed a security problem as well as a fear of rising unemployment, because 13% of all gainfully employed Maltese worked for British services.[77]

Thus Malta tried to find partners in addition to Britain in order to ensure its economic viability. One promising option was to establish close relations with the European Economic Community (EEC).[78] In 1967, Malta wrote to the Commission, that the small island desired to enter into negotiations about some kind of link or association.[79] Three years later an Association Agreement based on art. 238 TEC between the European Communities and Malta was signed, which came into force in 1971.[80] The agreement comprised two five-year-phases with the intention to achieve a customs union at the end of the second phase. It included factual free entry of industrial goods, tariff concessions on numerous traditional agricultural products, economic cooperation as well as financial assistance provided by the EC.[81] The governing Nationalist Party, being known for its pro-European attitude and being the driving force in this association process, was replaced in the 1971 general elections by the Malta Labour Party (MLP) which was rather opposed to the Nationalist Party's European policy. Thus, the success and the realisation of the agreement was partly contested right after its implementation:

> "The EU-Malta Association Agreement was, in fact, effectively stillborn. The pro-EU Nationalist government which negotiated it was replaced before it came into effect by an anti-EU Labour Government". (Redmond 1994, 9)

However, not all doubts and fears materialised. The Association Agreement, although hard to quantify, seemed to have had a positive effect on the Maltese economy. It seemed to be beneficial in facilitating economic growth and it "opened up the possibility for diversifying Malta's exports away from over reliance on the UK market and with increasing Malta's shares of the EC mar-

---

[77] Cf. Craig (1987), 172.

[78] Since 1967 referred to as European Community (EC) due to the merger of the three institutions EURATOM, EEC and ECSC.

[79] Cf. Federation of Industries Malta, 34.

[80] Cf. Bartholy (1989), 56.

[81] Ayres (1997), 3.

ket".[82] Furthermore, when the EC launched its *Global Mediterranean Policy* (GMP) in 1972, new protocols, which expanded the original Association Agreement with Malta by extending the first stage of the agreement to the end of 1980 plus further financial aid, were concluded.[83]

From a political point of view, the change in government also entailed a change in foreign policy. Instead of seeing the Association Agreement as one step in the direction of full membership, it was regarded by the Malta Labour Party and its charismatic leader Dom Mintoff as an economic tool to diminish the heavy dependence on Britain. Mintoff preferred a policy of mixed partners, i.e. not only directed towards the EC, but also directed towards establishing economic links with neighbours in the Mediterranean littoral and several Arab States.

The following events along with the Prime Minister's ambivalent policy behaviour further contributed to a first critical point in Malta-EU relations. The year 1980 passed by without an agreement reached between Malta and the EC on the second stage of the Association Agreement. In June 1981, Dom Mintoff proposed the launch of a "Special Relationship" to the European Community. In this "Special Relationship" proposal, Malta requested access to structural funds, free entry of agricultural products and no obligation to adopt the common customs tariff as intended by the EC within the scope of a second phase of the Association Agreement.[84] These far-reaching claims could have been interpreted by the EC as a consciously provocative act of this small island states, because "none of these demands are acceptable to the Community for they amount to the privileges of membership, without the accompanying burdens and duties".[85] Alarming signs concerning Malta's democratic situation and the development of a rather "anti-western" foreign policy aroused further suspicion by the EC. Enzo Rossi names in his study *Malta on the Brink:*

---

[82] Pace (2001), 154.

[83] Cf. Pace (2001), 146. The GMP was aimed to achieve free trade in manufactured goods between the EC and the Mediterranean countries through bilateral agreements.

[84] See Pace (1990), 12.

[85] Pace (1990), 12.

From Western Democracy to Libyan Satellite for example a drift from a pluralistic democracy to a system which is rather akin to the one-party regimes in Eastern Europe, violations of human rights and attacks on the freedom of press as alarming factors.[86] Rossi described Malta's policy at that time as a policy marked by "a total lack of commitment to Western Europe and a tendency to regard the Community as little more than a milch [*sic* milk] -cow for increasing levels of financial aid".[87]

The 1981 Maltese general elections resulted in the very unusual constellation in which the opposition, the Nationalist Party, obtained more votes than the governing Malta Labour Party, but the MLP managed to secure more parliamentary seats. As a consequence, the Nationalist Party did not participate in the plenary sessions for almost 1 ½ years.[88] During the Nationalist Party's boycott, the parliament passed the so called *Foreign Interference Act* which in principle forbade the participation of foreign politicians in political activities in Malta without permission from the Maltese government.[89] This law with its anti-democratic tendencies also contributed to aggravate the already tense atmosphere between the Maltese government and the EC.

The first phase of Malta-EU relations, after the island's independence and the retreat of the British troops, is thus marked by orientation, i.e. Malta's efforts to find strategic partners to ensure the island's economic survival and by deterioration in a political sense, namely rapidly changing foreign policy attitudes as well as a precarious domestic situation which marred the newly established relationship with the EC. Here it can already be seen that foreign policy attitudes and domestic decision-making issues are closely intertwined in Malta, perhaps closer than in larger countries. Narrow election results and the subsequent dispute between the Labour Party and the Nationalist Party, as well as the apparently very influential status of the respective Prime Minister, are issues which make it necessary to take a closer look at the Maltese

---

[86] Rossi (1986); cited in Pace (2001), 170.

[87] Rossi (1986); cited in Redmond (1993b), 26f.

[88] Pace (2001), 171f.

[89] Cf. Pace (2001), 174.

political culture and party system. This will assist with better understanding the Maltese domestic situation and the ongoing process of Malta-EU relations.

4.2. Malta's political culture and party system

Malta's political system is extraordinary in various aspects. Characteristics or specific features which have to be elucidated when discussing the Maltese political culture are high degrees of polarisation, personalisation and mobilisation as well as patron-client relationships and very high turnouts in general elections.

Since independence, power has alternated between the Nationalist Party and the Malta Labour Party.[90] The Nationalist Party (PN) or in Maltese *Partit Nazzjonalista* can be classed in the centre-right of the party spectrum with conservative tendencies and a strong affinity to the Catholic church. Members of the middle class are considered to be loyal PN voters. In contrast to the Nationalist Party, the democratic socialist Malta Labour Party (MLP) has a long tradition as a working class party with close links to the *General Workers' Union* (GWU). Though the boundaries of the parties' respective political standpoints have blurred a little over the last decades, there still exists a high level of antagonism between them.

Since the 1990s a third party called *Alternattiva Demokratika* (AD) has entered the Maltese political scene. The party can be regarded as Malta's Green Party. The popularity of this party has constantly increased, however the *Alternattiva Demokratika* has so far never won a seat in parliament. Thus, it is still justifiable to say that Malta has a de facto two-party system.

Another remarkable aspect in the island's political system is that election results tend to be very close. In the last three general elections, one of the parties always obtained slightly less than 50 percent of all votes and the other,

---

[90] Cf. Cini (2003b), 1.

consequently, a little more than 50 percent.[91] Although voting in Malta is not compulsory, the turnout in all three elections was well above 90 percent.[92] As a consequence, only a few thousand floating voters among the 280,000 registered decide who will govern the small island for the next five years.

How do these high turnouts and the narrow outcomes of election come about and how can they be explained? Polarisation, i.e. the division of the almost entire Maltese population in two political camps, represented by the Malta Labour Party and the Nationalist Party, is certainly an influential feature in Malta's political system. As Wolfgang Hirczy points out, this polarisation of the electorate is expressed by a confrontational style of electioneering, the stridency of the campaign rhetoric and mutual recrimination of party leaders and functionaries.[93]

Furthermore, politics in Malta is highly personalised. The party leader of the respective party is in the overall focus of attention and thus very influential. It can be observed that in Malta political leaders tend to remain in power for quite a long time. Prime examples for long terms of office are Dom Mintoff from the MLP and Dr Eddie Fenech Adami from the PN. Mintoff was Prime Minister from 1955 till 1958 and from 1971 to 1984. Dr Eddie Fenech Adami occupied the post from 1987 till 1996 and again from 1998 to 2004, and since has been the president of the island.[94] Due to this high degree of personalisation, besides political guidelines in party programmes, the leader's personal political view plays a dominant role in determining the party's general line, its decision-making processes and its policy behaviour.[95]

Polarisation and personalisation may help to explain the narrow outcome of election in Malta, but they only partly illuminate the phenomena of a regular

---

[91] General election 1996: MLP 50,70%, PN 47,80%, Others 1,5%; 1998: MLP 46,97%, PN 51,81%, Others 1,22%; 2003: MLP 47,51, PN 51,79, Others 0,7. Department of Information, Malta: http://www.doi.gov.mt/EN/elections/default.asp.

[92] Cf. Cini (2003b), 2.

[93] Hirczy (1995), 259.

[94] Cf. Department of Information, Malta: http://www.doi.gov.mt/EN/islands/lists/list6.asp.

[95] See also Bestler (2003), 156.

high turnout in general elections. Here mobilisation and patron-client relationships come into play. It has to be taken into consideration that in Maltese society there exists a pronounced social cohesion and social control, presumably more pronounced than in other (larger) societal groups. This social cohesion is likely to result from small size and insularity as external factors as well as strong family bonds and active local village communities as internal factors.[96]

In the run-up of an election the political actors actively start mobilising potential supporters.

> "Candidates go to great lengths in building their personal network of supporters, 'nursing' prospective constituencies for months before the election, holding public meetings, conducting house-to-house calls and seeking to establish themselves – or to reemphasize an already established position – as local patron, doing favours and trying to win friends." (Hirczy 1995, 263)

This concept of a local patron is also known as clientelism or patron-client relationships. As Anita Bestler points out patron-client relationships denote relationships in which individual party members are tied to their political group by personal relations to a political patron, often a member of parliament (MP). The patron is expected to do personal favours and in exchange, he can expect absolute loyalty and support from his client, normally expressed in the vote.[97]

After having outlined the inner dynamics and particularities of the Maltese political culture, it still needs to be clarified in how far they have an impact on Malta-EU relations. As mentioned before, domestic decision-making and foreign policy attitudes cannot be totally separated in Malta.

> "The PN and the MLP have always held conflicting positions on European integration. This has meant, somewhat unusually, that the dividing line between pro- and anti-Europeans in Malta has mapped relatively neatly onto pre-existing political cleavages." (Cini 2004, 586)

---

[96] Cf. Bartholy (1989), 41; Hirzcy (1995), 263.

[97] Bestler (2005), 156f.

As already mentioned[98], the Nationalist Party has been pro-European, whereas the Malta Labour Party has shown a rather anti-European attitude. These differing political attitudes have a major influence on the course of the development of Malta-EU relations. Furthermore, it should be kept in mind that the personal view of respective political leaders may also play a decisive role in the party's position towards the EU.

4.3. 1984 to 1992: Back on the road towards EU membership

After the troublesome start, signs of relaxation in Malta-EU relations could first be detected when, in 1984, Dom Mintoff handed over his Prime Ministerial post to Dr Karmenu Mifsud Bonnici who had in general a more pro-western attitude.[99] Thus, in 1985 a second financial protocol could be concluded and one year later the MLP government also expressed its desire to resume the political dialogue with the EC. These positive developments continued when the dispute between the two major Maltese parties could be settled with a change in the electoral law. A constitutional amendment provided that the party which obtained more than 50% of the votes would be entitled to co-opt sufficient additional seats in parliament to form a majority.[100] Furthermore, neutrality was inserted in the Maltese Constitution and the controversial clauses in the *Foreign Interference Act* were removed shortly before the 1987 general elections.[101]

On May 9 1987 the Nationalist Party returned to power, putting an end to 16 years of uninterrupted rule by the Malta Labour Party. Ironically, the newly introduced constitutional amendment ensured the Nationalist Party's election victory. The PN obtained 50.91% of all votes compared to 48.87% for the

---

[98] See 4.1. After Malta's Independence: orientation and deterioration.

[99] Cf. Bartholy (1989), 58.

[100] Fenech (1988), 133.

[101] The issue of Malta's neutrality will be discussed in detail later on.

Malta Labour Party, due to four co-opted members the Nationalist Party obtained 35 seats in parliament, one seat more than the MLP.[102]

After being elected to government, the Nationalist Party put much effort in reinstating Malta's international reputation and the government's credibility, as well as restoring the close links to the EC and pressing ahead a possible application for membership during the legislative period. The political dialogue with the Community was put on a new legal basis by prolonging the first phase of the Association Agreement once more to the end of 1990, to give Malta more time for reflection about the second stage and for further economic restructuring of the island.[103] Meanwhile the government introduced several economic reforms and started to set up necessary administrative structure for the preparation of the membership application. One measure was to appoint a so-called *Inter-Ministerial Committee on EC-Malta Relations* composed of members from different ministries whose task was to co-ordinate the efforts of the ministries on relations with the EC, and to compile the opinions of major economic and political actors concerning membership.[104] The plan was to wait for the right moment to launch the EU membership application.

The government's bustling activities concerning membership were not welcomed by all citizens, especially not by the opposition, as Dominic Fenech, a former general secretary of the MLP, underlines by at the same time defending the Labour Party's politics:

> "It remains to be seen whether the EEC will respond more generously to a government that wants to be a part of Europe at all costs. Labour Malta had seen itself as Mediterranean rather than European, seeking a role as a bridge between Europe to the north and the Arab countries to the south, thus complementing its policy of equidistance from East and West. It negotiated economic and security treaties with its immediate northern and southern neighbours, Italy and Libya. Above all, it objected to the Community's

[102] Cf. Fenech (1988), 133.

[103] From 1991 onwards a protocol ensured that the first stage of the Association Agreement was automatically extended from year to year. Cf. Pace (2001), 201.

[104] Cf. Bartholy (1989), 59f.; Pace (2001), 207.

> tendency to treat the Mediterranean as its backyard and, by implication, as unequal." (Fenech 1988, 136)

In 1988, while the Maltese government was still occupied with preparing the membership application, the European Parliament adopted a resolution on Malta and its relationship with the Community.[105] The resolution was based on a report prepared by the British MEP Derek Prag for the Political Affairs Committee. In the resolution the European Parliament seems to welcome Malta's aspirations for membership by stating that the European Parliament

> "wishes to see relations between Malta and the Community to become as close as possible eventually brough [*sic* brought] to the point at which, within suitable institutional arrangements, the Maltese people will be full participants in the Community." (Resolution on Malta, 2)

In this context it is important to note that in the motion for resolution on which the resolution is based on, the option for membership is not even mentioned:

> The European Parliament "wishes, within the framework of Association, to see relations between Malta and the Community become as close as possible." (Prag [n.d.], 6)

However, in the next paragraph of the resolution, the EP makes clear that membership might be a long-term option for Malta, but certainly not a near-future event, due to the past tensions and problems in the Malta-EU relationship:

> The European Parliament "believes that, in the light of the difficulties over the existing Association agreement which have arisen in the past, a new and closer Association agreement could provide a transitional solution and in particular create a stronger link between Malta and European Political Cooperation while remaining with the interests of the Community and the provisions of the Maltese constitution." (Resolution on Malta, 2)

The provision to which the resolution alludes to is the incorporation of neutrality in the Maltese constitution in 1987. The EC expressed its concerns that this provision might eventually pose problems regarding the European Political Cooperation:

---

[105] Resolution on Malta and its relationship with the European Community. No C 262/144, Doc. A2-128/88.

> "On the Community side, the difficulties might well prove to be the greatest in the political field. Many, perhaps a majority, of the twelve Member States would be anxious that Malta's policy of neutrality and non-alignment should not make agreement in European Political Cooperation even more difficult than it is already. The Twelve might wish to examine entirely new possible solutions: one such solution, for example, could be full membership of the three communities for Malta, but without the right of veto in EPC, or in certain aspects of EPC such as security." (Prag [n.d.], 18)

The Maltese government saw the resolution as a positive sign that Malta is on the right track. Finally in 1990, twenty years after the conclusion of the Association Agreement and after three years of preparation, the small island state launched its membership application, almost simultaneously with Cyprus, on July 16th.

But Malta and Cyprus were not the only countries applying for membership around that time. The EFTA members Austria, Finland and Sweden also filed their applications.[106] In 1992, the European Commission in preparation for the Lisbon European Council in July, published a document with the evocative title "Europe and the Challenge of Enlargement" to give a first response to all these applications.

The Commission came to the conclusion that the accession of the EFTA countries should be a feasible task:

> "The accession of the EFTA countries who have applied for membership - Austria, Sweden, Finland, and Switzerland - should not pose insuperable problems of an economic nature, and indeed would strengthen the Community in a number of ways".[107]

Regarding the other applicants, the Commission's first conclusion was more reluctant:

> "In the case of Malta and Cyprus, the adoption of the Community *acquis* would appear to pose no insuperable problems. However, both are very small States, and the question of their participation in the Community insti-

---

[106] Austria in 1989, Sweden in 1991 and Finland a few month before the Lisbon European Council in the year 1992.

[107] Europe and the Challenge of Enlargement, 24 June 1992, 18. (See Bibliography, Official EU Documents, for document number)

> tutions would have to be resolved in an appropriate manner in accession negotiations. The Commission will address this question in its Opinions on these countries' applications".[108]

The Lisbon European Council mainly followed the Commission's opinion by stating that accession negotiations with the EFTA countries can start as soon as the Treaty on European Union is ratified and a new financial agreement (Delors II package) is achieved.[109] For the Mediterranean applicants the Council avoided to give a precise timeline:

> "Relations with Cyprus and Malta will be developed and strengthened by building on the association agreements and their application for membership and by developing the political dialogue".[110]

With regard to these statements, it could already be discerned that the accession of the Mediterranean countries might still be delayed indefinitely. A twofold argument underlines this impression: Firstly, the European Union was very much occupied with inner reforms and restructuring, i.e. "deepening". Secondly, as far as "widening" of the EU was concerned, the EFTA members seemed to be better prepared for membership and much easier to handle in the eyes of the EU than the small Mediterranean island states Cyprus and Malta, whose accession would entail unique political, economic and institutional problems.

In this second phase of Malta-EU relations, a political redirection towards the west and a change in the Maltese government furthered a rapprochement between Malta and the European Union. Especially from the Maltese side, efforts were undertaken to establish closer links and to pave the way for EU membership. The European Union welcomed these new and promising developments, but at the same time remained cautious and a bit sceptical if the positive and pro-European trend in Malta would last. Thus, there were high expectations in Malta that the outstanding Commission's opinion on the Mal-

---

[108] Europe and the Challenge of Enlargement, 24 June 1992, 17f..

[109] Conclusion of the Presidency at the European Council, 23. (In the same document as footnote 106.)

[110] Conclusion of the Presidency at the European Council, 24. (Same document as footnote 106.)

tese application would clarify the situation and suggest definite steps on the road towards membership.

4.4. 1993 to 1999: Two Commission's opinions and two elections

In June 1993, three years after the application, the Commission finally published its opinion on Malta's application for membership. Positive on the surface and with concrete suggestions for Malta, but with no references to a fixed starting point of the negotiation process as a prerequisite for an early accession, the Commission's opinion only met partly with Malta's expectations.

Concerning the political sphere the issue of Malta's neutrality was picked up again and this time the EU formulated its doubts more precisely than in the Prag Report:[111]

> "The principle of neutrality and of Malta's non-aligned status set out in the Maltese Constitution raise the problem of their compatibility with Title V of the Maastricht Treaty and could lead to difficulties in the area of 'joint action' and future cooperation on defence."[112]

However, for the Maltese government, Malta's neutrality was not perceived as an obstacle towards EU membership, since, as the Nationalist Party argued, the Maltese neutrality and non-alignment relates exclusively to neutrality in a military sense and simply prohibits the use or deployment of military bases, facilities or personnel on the island.[113] Other countries, for example Austria, could serve as role-models concerning the treatment of neutral states in the EU.[114]

Furthermore, the Commission alluded to the institutional problems in connection with Malta's small size:

---

[111] Cf. 4.3. 1984 to 1992: Back on the road towards EU membership, page 39 in this study.

[112] The challenge of enlargement. Commission opinion on Malta's application for membership, Bulletin of the European Communities, Supplement 4/93, 10.

[113] Cf. Redmond (1994a), 140.

> "Malta has only a very few senior public officials with sufficient international experience to play a full part in the decision-making and operational processes of the Community institutions. (...) Another question that has to be asked in the light of the above is whether Malta would, in the foreseeable future, be able to take on the wide range of responsibilities and obligations incumbent on the Presidency of the Council."[115]

The Commission proposed to raise the institutional questions again in a more general context during the next intergovernmental conference in 1996.

As far as the economic sphere is concerned, the Commission asserted that the transition required to integrate Malta into the community has been made more difficult by the fact that the second stage of the Association Agreement, i.e. the creation of a customs union, did not proceed.[116] Consequently, the Commission urged Malta to undertake a wide range of necessary economic reforms with conviction and continuity, because otherwise accession negotiations could not start:

> "The reforms which imply Malta's adoption of the *acquis communautaire* affect so many different areas (tax, finance, movement of capital, trade protection, competition law etc.) and require so many changes in traditional patterns of behaviour that what is effectively involved is a root-and-branch overhaul of the entire regulatory and operational framework of the Maltese economy."[117]

Thus, the Maltese government was now under pressure to put through these extensive and rather unpopular economic reforms in a short period of time in order to fulfil the conditions of membership laid down by the European Union.

Nevertheless, the government was still convinced that membership was the right option for the small island state, not only from a political and economic

---

[114] Cf. Pace (2001), 245.

[115] The challenge of enlargement. Commission opinion on Malta's application for membership, Bulletin of the European Communities, Supplement 4/93, 14.

[116] Cf. Commission opinion on Malta's application for membership, Bulletin of the European Communities, Supplement 4/93, 11.

[117] Commission opinion on Malta's application for membership, Bulletin of the European Communities, Supplement 4/93, 13.

point of view, but also in terms of security as the Prime Minister Dr Eddie Fenech Adami pointed out in 1994:

> "We live in a dangerous sea. We have always lived in it. Yet today we have the opportunity of anchoring our country to an emerging political union which shares our moral values, our Christian culture and our beliefs in democracy, the rule of law and social justice. We see the EU gaining strength and cohesion, being endowed with its common foreign policy and tomorrow, perhaps, with its common security policy.
>
> Malta's security is the first aim of our foreign policy, and it is in our interest to belong to an entity which makes us more secure." (Speech of Prime Minister, cited in Pace 2001, 200)

Here Fenech Adami alludes to the "security dilemma" of small states and their strategic actions to secure their survival. Malta's security policy after independence was based on neutrality and non-alignment, but in the course of the years it became clear that this concept has lost much of its influential power, thus membership in a supranational organisation was seen as an adequate substitution to ensure the state's survival. In the eyes of the governing Nationalist Party, at least.

To give the Maltese people a positive signal and to no longer keep the small island state guessing about the timeline for membership, in 1995 the Cannes European Council stated that the formal pre-accession dialogue with Malta and Cyprus would start six months after the 1996 Intergovernmental Conference (IGC).[118] However, this fixed starting point could not be met due to internal policy changes in Malta, causing another delay on the island's way towards EU membership.

The general elections in Malta, which took place in October 1996, returned the Malta Labour Party to power after nine years of opposition.[119] The MLP had campaigned against EU membership, favouring again the creation of special links with the European Union. In its electoral manifesto the MLP stated that it would neither stand up for membership nor for a customs union,

---

[118] Cf. Baldacchino (2002), 200.

[119] This election, in line with the previous ones, was marked by a very close outcome, resulting in 35 seats in parliament for the MLP and 34 seats for the PN.

but it would seek to conclude some sort of a free trade agreement with the European Union including cooperation in several other policy fields as well. The party went on arguing that membership meant to adopt EU policies which are designed for large countries and which do not take into consideration the needs of small states like Malta.[120] Thus, the newly elected Prime Minister Dr Alfred Sant did not hesitate to make clear that "for the foreseeable future we are ruling out the prospect of Maltese membership of the EU in the full belief that on a net basis, such membership would not be in the interest neither of Malta nor of Europe".[121]

In contrast to the former PN government, Sant and his party regarded Malta's neutrality as a vital and significant concept in the Maltese security policy, especially concerning the developments in the Mediterranean region. The Prime Minister envisioned Malta as a little "Switzerland in the Mediterranean", meaning that Malta's security could best be safeguarded by maintaining a position where it will pose a threat to no one in the Mediterranean, neither in the North nor in the South.[122]

To underline the new Maltese foreign policy agenda, the Maltese government promptly suspended the EU membership application in November 1996. The "freezing" of the application denotes the second low point in Malta-EU relations and it is again closely linked to Malta's domestic situation and its virtual two-party system. The European Union reacted to these developments by proposing to carry on the relations on the basis of the 1970 Association Agreement and under the framework of the Euro-Mediterranean Partnership.

But once again, political developments in Malta led to a redirection of Malta-EU relations. In 1998, after only 22 months in office, Dr Alfred Sant called for early elections in a bid to win a stable parliamentary majority. The MLP had a one-seat majority in parliament, but due to the defection of a member of

[120] Cf. Pace (2001), 267.

[121] Speech by Dr Alfred Sant delivered at the Chamber of Commerce, cited in Pace (2001), 265-266.

[122] See also Pace (2001), 265.

Sant's own party on some key votes, Sant's position had been undermined.[123] Strangely enough, the MLP member who had voted against his party was Dom Mintoff, the former MLP Prime Minister whose anti-western policy attitudes in the 1970s and 1980s had been the catalyst for the first tensions in Malta-EU relations. The Malta Labour Party lost the general elections and the Nationalist Party was re-elected with 51,8% of all votes, resulting in a comfortable lead – from a Maltese point of view - of a five seat majority in parliament.[124]

One of the first official acts of Dr Eddie Fenech Adami as Prime Minister was to immediately reactivate Malta's EU membership application. This reactivation constitutes a unique occurrence in the history of EU enlargements.[125] Due to the membership reactivation, the European Commission was asked by the Council to present an updated report on Malta's application. This report was already published in February 1999. In the report the Commission confirmed that the required economic reforms as laid down in the 1993 Commission's opinion had largely been implemented.

> "Malta is a functioning market economy, and should be able to cope with competitive pressure and market forces within the Union provided it takes the appropriate measures, in particular by continued industrial restructuring. The main challenge for economic policy in Malta in the next few years is to bring down the government deficit and to enforce the collection of government revenue. Malta should also continue to open up its economy by further trade and capital account liberalisation. It should persist in the strengthening and implementation of the economic policies undertaken by the Government."[126]

Concerning the political sphere the Commission stated that as far as democracy, rule of law, and human rights are concerned, Malta fulfils the Copen-

---

[123] Cf. BBC News, September 6, 1998.

[124] Cf. Calleya (2000).

[125] See also European Parliament: Briefing No. 5 Malta and Relations with the European Union, PE 167/350/rev. 4, 7.

[126] 1999 Regular Report from the Commission on Malta's Progress Towards Accession, 16.

hagen criteria and thus the screening process with Malta should start as soon as possible.[127]

This phase evidently shows some analogies to the first phase of Malta-EU relations. A pro-European government tries to conduct the country as fast as possible on the road towards EU-membership, but a change in government leads to a u-turn of this process and causes tensions between the small island state and the EU. The effects of membership for such a small state like Malta are difficult to predict and there exists a high polarisation on the issue of membership. It once again becomes clear that the influence of a single political leader in Malta should not be underestimated. It also becomes clear that the European Union is certainly not willing to comply with all demands of a tiny Mediterranean island state whose foreign policy attitudes may change faster than the EU can react. Despite the difficulties and delays in this phase of Malta-EU relations, the small island state seems to be closer to membership than ever:

> "The Commission expects that, at that juncture, when the European Council discusses the possibility of extending the accession negotiations, Malta will be able to join the candidate countries with which negotiations are already underway."[128]

4.5. Alternatives to EU membership

The European Union has finally opened the door for the small island state of Malta to become a part of a powerful regional organisation. EU membership entails far-reaching implications for Malta which are difficult to assess. Thus, before trying to weigh the advantages and disadvantages of membership itself, it is also advisable to take a look at possible or at least conceivable alternatives of EU membership for Malta. One option could be to expand and intensify existing relations with Malta's southern, non-European neighbours in the Mediterranean region. When concentrating on Europe, but having in mind

---

[127] 1999 Regular Report from the Commission on Malta's Progress Towards Accession, 9.

[128] 1999 Regular Report from the Commission on Malta's Progress Towards Accession, 4.

a more loose cooperation, other options such as a free trade area agreement or a customs union between Malta and the EU need to be briefly discussed in this context.

4.5.1. European integration or Mediterranean collaboration?

Throughout the decades, due to Malta's geographical position, the island seemed to be wavering between becoming a fully integrated part of Europe, or pursuing and deepening the traditional good relations with its North African neighbours in the Mediterranean littoral. With Malta's application for EU membership, a final decision was taken in favour of Europe. What are the reasons and considerations behind this decision and what does it reveal about Malta's vision concerning her role in the world?

For Malta, the question "Europe or Africa" is not so much related to identity, because, despite noticeable Arabic influences, for example in the Maltese language, the Maltese have stressed their affiliation to Europe over and over again. The question is more of an economic nature. Though the European Union has been Malta's largest trading partner, the small island state has always fostered with great care its economic links with North Africa, especially with the oil exporting country Libya, arousing suspicion in European circles:

> "Under the longstanding leadership of Dom Mintoff (...) the ties to North Africa, and especially Libya, were nurtured to the extent of raising suspicion in the Western media of Malta being 'a Libyan Trojan Horse'. For most of the period of Maltese independence the idea that Malta could serve as a 'gateway' to North Africa has figured prominently, especially among those who have an alternate vision for Malta's future than membership of the European Union". (Magnússon [n.d.], 3)

However, deeper integration with one or several North African states or countries in the Middle East seems to be highly problematic for Malta, because the smooth functioning of cooperative structures between a group of states is rare[129] partly due high protectionist barriers and the tense political and economic atmosphere in this region:

> "Today there is *quasi* unanimous consensus that the major threats to security in the Mediterranean are of a non-military nature. Most of the states of the southern Mediterranean littoral are concerned with internal security issues widely related to the possibility of state collapse because of the deteriorating economic situation and the protest against leading political elites in each country (...)." (Pace 1997, 12)

Hence, despite Malta's proximity to the North African and Middle East markets, Mediterranean collaboration as a substitute to EU membership has never been seriously contemplated in Malta.

This does not necessarily mean that Malta abandons her traditionally good relations with North Africa when joining the EU. Malta envisions that as a member of the European Union the small island state could utilise relations by taking over the function as a tiny, but highly significant connecting link between Europe and North Africa. Thus, Malta might serve as a "stepping stone" to North Africa or the island may even develop into a hub in the Mediterranean region, a position which, from a Maltese point of view, would in the long term be profitable for Malta, for the EU and for the non-European Mediterranean countries.

4.5.2. Free Trade Area Agreement or Customs Union

The European Union is Malta's largest trading partner and the Maltese government is aware that access to EU markets is a major pillar in ensuring the small island's economic survival.[130] Accession to the European Union means radical economic reforms for Malta and the question which has to be posed in this context is: Is EU membership the one and only possible solution for Malta or do other comparably effective, but less "painful" alternatives exist?

---

[129] One exception is the Agadir Agreement signed in 2004 by Jordan, Tunisia, Morocco and Egypt with the aim to establish a free trade area until 2010.

[130] Trade with the EU accounts for 63.6% of total imports and 47.8% of total exports in 2001, cf. Bayar (2003), 40.

One alternative to full membership could be the creation of a customs union between Malta and the EU as originally envisaged in the 1970 Association Agreement. The main characteristic of a customs union is the Common External Tariff. A customs union might increase the economic efficiency of the member countries and it may lead to closer political ties. However, in the case of Malta, a customs union seems to be a less advantageous solution in comparison to membership. It would cause considerable difficulties for the less competitive elements of Maltese economy and would reduce Maltese revenues, as the current tariffs would have to be replaced by the lower common external tariff of the EU.[131] Although Malta would receive more financial help than under the Association Agreement, it could not reap the benefits full membership would bring, e.g. access to structural funds, agricultural subsidies and participation in the EU decision-making processses.[132] Consequently, it can be stated that in the case of Malta, a customs union is no adequate substitute to membership.

Another option would be an even more loose cooperation in the form of a free trade area agreement. Such a bilateral agreement would include the elimination of tariffs and quotas on goods circulating between Malta and the EU, but without a common external tariff. The Maltese Ministry for Economic Services concluded in a study on Malta's National Industrial Policy in 2003 that, like a customs union,

> "a free-trade agreement would carry the same adjustment burdens as economic union, without the financial and other benefits of the latter. A free-trade agreement would keep Malta shut out of the EU deliberative process, outside the making of the EU decisions that determine the nation's livelihood." (Ministry for Economic Services, 25-26)

Especially, in connection with the EU accession of other countries, a Maltese solo attempt with a free trade agreement would be detrimental:

> "The option of entering a free trade agreement with the EU does not provide a secure and broad platform for Malta to blossom as a destination for FDI

---

131 Redmond (1993a), 104.

132 Cf. Redmond (1994), 8 and Redmond (1993a), 104.

> [*foreign direct investment*] and as a node of economic activity. This is particularly true when other countries, like Cyprus and the nations of Central and Eastern Europe, will soon become members. As these countries move closer to membership, for Malta to stay out would be outright perilous." (Ministry for Economic Services, 26)

Furthermore, as an EU member Malta could profit from all trade agreements the EU has with other countries. As a non-member, Malta would have to negotiate individual agreements from the weak and isolated position of a small Mediterranean island state.[133]

A third option, favoured and concretised by the Malta Labour Party would be the already mentioned 'Special Relationship':

> "It involves a long-term (fifteen to twenty years) agreement leading eventually to a Malta-EC industrial free trade zone but involving political and technical cooperation (such as Maltese participation in the EC's research and development programmes) from the onset. In addition, Malta would continue to have preferential access to the EC market and would receive substantial financial assistance." (Redmond 1993a, 104)

As stated earlier in this study[134], the EU would not be willing to grant a small Mediterranean island state such a special status which comprises the privileges of membership without the corresponding obligations and duties.

After having taken into consideration possible alternatives to membership, it becomes clear that these options could be attractive for a short period of time. The economic transformation needed is not as far-reaching as in a membership context, but in the long run, EU membership seems to be the only promising solution to ensure the island's economic prosperity:

> "EU enlargement is an historical opportunity and challenge for Malta. The European Union will widen and the pan-Euro-Mediterranean integration will continue to develop whether Malta joins or not. However, staying out means an increasing gap in living standards, growth, and prosperity between Malta and the rest of Europe. The enlarged European Union will represent 20% of world output, 25% of world trade, 65% of world monetary reserves with a

---

[133] Cf. Ministry for Economic Services, 25.

[134] Cf. 4.1. After Malta's Independence: orientation and deterioration.

structural surplus of €130 billion in trade and high technology industries and services. Can Malta afford not to form part of this reality?" (Bayar 2003, 90)

4.6. 1999 to 2004: Negotiations, Referendum and Accession Process

After the unique situation in the history of EU enlargement of Malta reactivating her membership application and the publication of the Commission's updated report on Malta's application in February 1999, the official screening process with Malta could start in May 1999. In this context, the Maltese government was also asked to prepare a National Programme for the Adoption of the *acquis* (NPAA). The screening process precedes the actual negotiation process in order to compare a candidate's and EU legislation with the aim of highlighting the differences between the two. Where major differences emerge, it is probable that long and tough negotiations might follow.[135]

In December 1999, the Helsinki European Council invited Romania, Slovakia, Latvia, Lithuania, Bulgaria and Malta to join the negotiation process already underway with the so called *Luxembourg group* consisting of Poland, Hungary, the Czech Republic, Estonia, Slovenia and Cyprus.[136] Then, on 15th February 2000, the European Union gave the green light for the start of individual accession negotiations with the *Helsinki group*, including Malta.

Finally, after many ups and downs in Malta-EU relations, the small Mediterranean island state could start negotiating with the European Union about accession. The Maltese Foreign Minister Joseph Borg declared that after all these years, Malta is ready and prepared to join the EU. He went on stating that "the start of negotiations marks a 'truly historic day' for his country and that the government will spare no effort to ensure that Malta catches up with

---

[135] Cf. Bayar (2003), 55.

[136] Cf. European Parliament: Briefing No. 5 Malta and Relations with the European Union, PE 167/350/rev. 4, 16.

the 'Luxembourg group' countries, so as to be part of the first wave of accessions".[137]

Concerning the financial aid, embedded in the pre-accession strategy granted by the European Union, a Council regulation for Cyprus and Malta specifies the conditions for and the amount of financial aid. Article 2 of this regulation states:

> "(...) for a period expiring on 31 December 2004, the financial reference amount for the implementation of this Regulation shall be EUR 95 million. The annual appropriations shall be authorised by the budgetary authority within the limits of the financial perspectives".[138]

Malta will receive 38 million € out of the total 95 million € pre-accession aid designated for the two Mediterranean islands over a five-year period.[139]

During the negotiations of the 31 chapters belonging to the *acquis communautaire* between February 2000 and December 2002, Malta managed to obtain 76 special arrangements in 13 sectors.[140] Many of them are transitional agreements in sensitive fields of Malta's economy. As Ali Bayar observes:

> "These requests were clearly made with the aim of avoiding sudden shocks to the economy in general (as in the case of free movement of people) or to specific sectors such as the ship building sector were a transitional period for the gradual removal of subsidies was negotiated." (Bayar 2003, 55)

In comparison to the other aspirant countries, the tiny Mediterranean island was very successful in putting through its requests, because Malta managed to negotiate the second largest number of transitional agreements after Poland.[141]

---

[137] European Parliament: Briefing No. 5 Malta and Relations with the European Union, PE 167/350/rev. 4, 17.

[138] Council Regulation (EC) No 555/2000 of 13 March 2000.

[139] Cf. <http://www.delmlt.cec.eu.int/eu_assistance/financial_cooperation.htm>

[140] Cf. Aġġornat, Weekly bulletin published by the Malta-EU Information Centre, No. 156, December 2002, 1.

[141] Cf. Tables in Lippert (2004), 53 and Lippert (2003), 4.

Numerous transitional agreements and special arrangements are linked to Malta's small size, population density and insularity.

Concerning the free movement of persons, Malta expressed the concern that after accession, unemployment would be likely to increase as the small Maltese labour market might be flooded by an influx of non-Maltese EU nationals. To avoid such a sudden influx of foreign workers, Malta negotiated a transitional provision according to which for the first seven years after date of membership, Malta may impose restrictions unilaterally in urgent and exceptional cases where the influx of workers from the EU creates pressure on the local labour market or particular sectors. If the problem still exists after the expiration of seven years, the EU and Malta will talk about possible remedies.[142]

In chapter four "Free movement of capital", Malta negotiated an arrangement in which the island may maintain restrictions on a non-discriminatory basis, on the right of EU citizens who have not legally resided in Malta for at least five years to acquire and hold secondary residences. Normally, according to the *acquis*, "property would have had to be made available for purchase without any restrictions to all EU nationals"[143]. Due to Malta's image as being an attractive holiday location with favourable climate, many EU-nationals might have thought about buying property there as a second residence, after the island's EU accession. Here Malta's smallness comes into play again, since due to the very limited land available for construction purposes, such a provision would certainly have led to an enormous increase in property prices.[144]

Furthermore, although Malta's agricultural sector is insignificant in EU terms, Malta insisted on *Special Market Policy Programme for Maltese Agriculture*.

> This programme "takes into account the realities of the local scenario and provides for special temporary state aid for farmers (...) to enable them to

[142] Cf. Buttigieg (2004), 4; Aġġornat, Weekly bulletin published by the Malta-EU Information Centre, No. 156, December 2002, 1.

[143] Buttigieg (2004), 5.

[144] Cf. Buttigieg (2004), 4f.

> adapt to the changes in the market environment resulting from the dismantlement of the levies." (Buttigieg 2004, 6)

As far as the small-scale Maltese fishery sector is concerned, Malta successfully negotiated a coastal area agreement in which Malta was granted a 25-mile coastal zone exclusively accessible for Maltese fishermen.[145]

The issue of Malta's neutrality, which had already come up several times in the past, was now laid down in the form of a declaration confirming that Malta's neutrality is not affected by membership.[146]

Not only measures to safeguard the small Maltese economy were negotiated, but also specific national interests were addressed by Malta. For example, due to the pronounced Catholicism, Malta is one of the few countries in which divorce is still forbidden and not legalised. Thus, the EU had to accept that concerning matrimonial matters, relevant EU Conventions need not apply to Malta in cases of particular concordats with the Vatican. Another, rather controversial particularity is bird hunting and trapping in Malta. The island insisted on a derogation whereby Maltese hunters can continue to go bird hunting in spring.[147]

Why was the small Mediterranean island state, whose political powers are - according to theoretical findings – rather limited, able to obtain so many special arrangements and transitional periods? Was the EU impressed by Malta's negotiation skills or was the EU more willing to give concessions to such a small and rather insignificant candidate than for larger aspirant

countries such as Hungary or the Czech Republic? Many factors come into play during such extensive negotiations and the reasons for particular decisions cannot always be traced back. At least it can be stated that Malta, like other economically weak candidate countries, obtained necessary and helpful transitional arrangements in sensitive economic fields to cushion the impact

---

[145] Cf. Walker/ Elliott (2004), 180.

[146] Cf. EPP-ED www.epp-ed.org/Press/pdoc03/accession_treaty-mt.doc

[147] Cf. Aġġornat, Weekly bulletin published by the Malta-EU Information Centre, No. 156, December 2002, 3.

of accession. In other fields, which are significant for Malta, but of minor importance to the European Union in general, the EU could shorten negotiations by granting concessions.

Throughout the negotiation process, regular reports were published by the European Commission to monitor the progress of each candidate country. All reports have a similar structure. Firstly, relations between the candidate and the EU are described, followed by an analysis concerning the fulfilment of the political and economic criteria set by the 1993 Copenhagen European Council.[148] Secondly, the Commission looks at the candidate's capacity to assume the obligations of membership, meaning the adoption of the whole *acquis communautaire.*

Concerning the political sphere, the Commission pointed out in the 2001 Progress Report on Malta that

> "Malta continues to fulfil the Copenhagen political criteria. Further efforts have been made to prepare the administration for operation within the EU, and the authorities' record on democratic and human rights remains generally good. There has been further progress as regards the functioning of the justice system with the reduction of the backlog of judiciary cases and preliminary steps have been taken to implement the Refugees Act." (2001 Regular Report, 16)

The macroeconomic developments in Malta were also judged as being quite satisfying in terms of GDP growth, unemployment, inflation and reduction of the government deficit. However, the Commission remarked that "despite the decreasing trend, the fiscal deficit remains too high, contributing further to a very large current account deficit. Although the current account deficit had a strong one-off component, it will need to be closely monitored. The authorities need to put public finances in a sustainable medium-term path".[149]

Regarding financial support from the EU, 38 million € total pre-accession aid was provided for the period 2000-2004, of which 7.5 million € were allocated

---

[148] For example, democracy, rule of law, human rights protection, functioning market economy and the capacity to cope with competitive pressures and markets forces within the EU are part of the Copenhagen criteria.

[149] 2001 Regular Report on Malta's Progress Towards Accession, 27.

to Malta in the year 2001 for projects in Justice and Home Affairs, Regional Policy, Social Policy, Customs and Tax, Education, Standards and Administrative Cooperation.[150]

Shortly after the Commissions Report, the Maltese Ministry of Foreign Affairs published its updated *National Programme for the Adoption of the Acquis* in January 2002. The National Programme, among other concrete measures, presented a plan aiming at dismantling all levies on EU imported products by 2003, excluding agricultural products.[151]

Later that year in October, the Commission submitted the annual progress report in which Malta's good performance in the political sphere was reaffirmed, but problems were again identified in the economic sphere and specific suggestion were made:

> "Further improvements can be made to macroeconomic management by reducing the general government deficit and reforming public expenditure to ensure medium-term fiscal sustainability. More progress can be made on restructuring large loss-making public enterprises and public utilities. Attention should be paid to the supervision of nonperforming loans in the banking sector." (2002 Regular Report, 34)

The pre-accession aid allocated to Malta in that year amounted to 9.5 million Euro for projects in Environment, Agriculture, Fisheries, Maritime Safety, Public Health, Transport, Education and general Technical Assistance.[152]

Subsequently, the Commission forwarded the progress report to the European Parliament with the request to issue an opinion concerning every candidate country. As far as Malta is concerned, in contrast to the Commission, the European Parliament did not refer to the island's economic situation, but it expressed its concerns about the uncertain domestic political situation in Malta:

> "Regarding domestic politics, nothing has changed in the Labour Party's fundamental opposition to Maltese accession to the EU, and it is likewise

[150] 2001 Regular Report on Malta's Progress Towards Accession, 6.

[151] Malta: National Programme for the Adoption of the Acquis (NPAA), 23.

[152] 2002 Regular Report on Malta's Progress Towards Accession, 11.

> unclear what attitude the party would take to a future referendum on EU membership. (...) There has, however, been one new development in the political situation in Malta because the former Prime Minister Dom Mintoff has launched his own campaign, which is not intrinsically hostile to the EU, but critical first and foremost of the results achieved by the Government in the negotiations. The outcome of an EU referendum once the negotiations have been completed is therefore uncertain. However, Maltese citizens should realise that Malta will not be given a third chance." (European Parliament: Report on enlargement, 39)

With unusual clear words, the EP emphasised that if the domestic political situation drifted again into a rather anti-European direction, as it had happened in the past, Malta would not be offered another chance to become a full member of the European Union.

The formally consultative, but in reality quasi binding referendum on EU membership, mentioned in the EP's resolution, took place on 8th March 2003. The referendum question was: "Do you agree that Malta becomes member of the European Union in the enlargement that will take place on 1st May 2004?"[153] In the run-up to the referendum a "Yes" and a "No" camp emerged with the governing Nationalist Party in the "Yes" camp and the Malta Labour Party as driving force behind the "No" camp. This polarisation exactly mirrors the parties' attitudes towards the EU throughout the last forty years. Further backing for the "Yes" movement came from the *Alternattiva Demokratika* (AD), Malta's small green party, the *Federation of Industries* (FOI), the *Confederation of Trade Unions* and even Malta's English language newspapers, *Times of Malta* and *Malta Independent*, adopted an "unashamedly pro-EU stance".[154] Next to the MLP, the *General Workers' Union*, Malta's largest trade union, and some pro-Labour media, e.g. the 'Super 1' TV channel, constituted the "No" camp.[155]

A very heated campaign, marked by "legal wrangling over names appearing on the electoral register" and "accusations of anti-democratic behaviour and

---

[153] Bestler (2005), 167.

[154] Cf. Cini (2004), 588.

[155] Cf. Cini (2003a), 3.

outright lying thrown about by both camps" followed.[156] The "pro EU-movement" argued that Malta was a country with a European identity and that the small island state could only develop further as part of a larger bloc, namely the EU, in order to be able to compete in a globalised world.[157]

The "contra-movement" warned that due to EU membership food prices would rise, foreigners would buy Maltese property and take away the jobs of the Maltese, although these fears had already been largely taken into account by the Maltese government during the special arrangements negotiations. The MLP leader Alfred Sant went on arguing that besides the shock for the Maltese economy, Malta would be too small for EU structures and the island would risk to lose its Mediterranean identity.[158] Sant even called on the Maltese citizens to either vote "no", to abstain by registering, but not voting, or to invalidate the ballot paper by writing 'Viva Malta' on it. He himself abstained on the day of the referendum.[159]

The official final result of the referendum was 53.65 % (143,094) for the "Yes" camp and 46.35 % (123,628) for "No". Around 3,900 votes (1.45 %) were invalid.[160] The turnout was again very high, but not unusual for Malta, at 91%. Thus, after the announcement of the result, the pro EU-membership camp celebrated its referendum victory due to a narrow majority of only 20.000 votes. The following day, Prime Minister Adami took advantage of this favourable pro-European result and called for general elections on 12 April 2003, four days before the planned signing of the Accession Treaty in Athens.[161] The general elections in April confirmed the pro-European policy of the government, since the governing Nationalist Party obtained 51.79% of all votes

---

[156] Cini (2003a), 2.

[157] See also Bestler (2005), 167.

[158] Cf. Cini (2004), 590; Bestler (2005), 168.

[159] Cini (2003a), 3f.

[160] Referendum, final result cf. <http://www.gov.mt/frame.asp?l=2&url=http://www.doi.gov.mt>

[161] Cini (2003b), 2.

compared to 47.51 % for the Malta Labour Party.[162] The turnout of 96.2% was remarkable, even in Maltese terms.[163] With this pro-European mandate of the Maltese citizens "in his luggage," the old and new Prime Minister Dr Eddie Fenech Adami flew to Athens to sign Malta's EU Accession Treaty.

In September 2003, the Commission published its last monitoring report on Malta before accession. Since ambiguities in the political sphere had been largely settled and since after the referendum and the general elections a sudden change in Malta's pro-European policy behaviour was not to be expected in the near future, the Commission focused in the report on Malta's remaining problems in the economic sphere. Although the Commission approved Malta's progress in various fields, it voiced its concerns about the island's macroeconomic situation: "Economic activity remained weak, affected by low external demand and the downturn in the tourism sector. Progress with structural reforms has been mixed."[164] Furthermore, the government deficit, outlined in the previous reports, still posed a problem:

> "Much needed in-depth reforms which allow for long-term savings are lacking. Achieving fiscal consolidation is necessary to face critical challenges ahead, as the public finances are expected to remain significantly constrained by demographic developments and investment needs required to comply with EU standards and catching up with EU income per capita levels".[165]

The Commission addressed the problematic issue of the high Maltese government deficit (9.7 % of GDP in 2003) again in its recommendation on the broad guidelines of the economic policies of the member states and the community:

> "In a context of little efforts to consolidate public finances, lower than expected GDP growth in 2003 and mounting public expenditure have further deteriorated the general government deficit, placing pressure on the current account balance. Policies in Malta should pursue a high degree of sustain-

---

[162] Department of Information, Malta. General Election Results.

[163] Cf. Cini (2003b), 2.

[164] Comprehensive monitoring report on Malta's preparations for membership 2003, 52.

[165] Comprehensive monitoring report on Malta's preparations for membership 2003, 7f.

able convergence, in particular as regards the consolidation of public finances."[166]

Thus, the Commission defined three key priorities areas in which Malta needed to catch up prior to accession. The first priority was to ensure a reduction of the general government deficit on a sustainable basis and the long-term sustainability of public finances. Secondly, efforts to increase employment rates, especially among women, should be undertaken and thirdly, the Maltese government should encourage effective competition taking into account the specific characteristics of the small domestic economy.[167]

Concerning financial aid in 2003, an amount of €12.68 million was committed for projects in the Environment, Agriculture and Rural Development, Maritime Safety, Road and Transport, Data Protection, Justice and Home Affairs with particular reference to Border Control, the continual support in Customs and Taxation, Participation in Community Programmes and Agencies and general Technical Assistance.[168]

Shortly after Malta's accession to the European Union on May 1st 2004, the citizens of the small island state were asked once more to go to the polls, this time to elect Malta's five representatives in the European Parliament elections taking place on June 12th. 27 candidates ran for the elections, respectively eight candidates from the Nationalist Party and the Malta Labour Party, one candidate from Malta's green party and 10 independent candidates.[169] With an ironic undertone, the Maltese professor Roderick Pace describes the election campaign as follows:

> "The issues in this campaign consisted of a rich, fruity 'Macedonia' of domestic and EU issues mixed with American campaign-style attacks on the credibility of some of the candidates, with sporadic anti-clericalism and anti-

---

[166] Commission Recommendation on the 2004 update of the Broad Guidelines of the Economic Policies of the Member States and the Community, 46.

[167] Commission Recommendation on the 2004 update of the Broad Guidelines of the Economic Policies of the Member States and the Community, 46.

[168] Cf. http://www.delmlt.cec.eu.int./eu_assistance/financial_cooperation.htm.

[169] Cf. Bestler (2005), 171.

> Catholicism and not excluding a few racist diatribes for good measure." (Pace 2004, 4)

As far as arguments are concerned, the pro-European Nationalist Party underlined that if their candidates were elected, they would form part of the largest political group within the European Parliament, namely the European People's Party (EPP), which would enhance Malta's ability to put through national aims within an EU context.[170] The governing PN also tried to distract the voters from the still problematic economic situation on the island and recently taken unpopular reform measures in the health sector Malta's dockyards.

Many Maltese had hoped that the island's situation would improve immediately after accession and now they began to show their disappointment, which was mirrored in the election result. The MLP managed to obtain three of the five seats in the European Parliament and the PN only two. A turnout around 81 % was more than satisfactory for the EU, but low in Maltese terms.[171]

This phase of Malta-EU relations from the year 1999 to 2004 finally culminates in Malta's accession to the European Union. Malta put a lot of effort into demonstrating that the small island state was not only willing to join the EU, but also ready and prepared to fulfil the accession criteria. A pro-European atmosphere was noticeable in Malta, although the EU-referendum and the following general election showed that political polarisation on the island has in no way diminished. As pointed out in several Commission reports, Malta's economic situation was still a cause for concern. Financial aid from the EU can be seen as one way to stabilise the Maltese economy, but as Roderick Pace rightly emphasises:

> "In our approach to Europe we must banish from our minds the thought that membership of the Community is a cure at all, that all we have to do is sit it out and our economy moves up the development ladder on its own. The

---

[170] Cf. Pace (2004), 5.

[171] Cf. Bestler (2005), 175.

> benefits of membership could easily be squandered by the adoption of the wrong set of domestic policies." (Pace 1990, 14)

Due to Malta's smallness and the close connection between domestic and foreign policy issues on the island, it may be even more important that political decision-makers pay special attention to specific needs of Malta's small scale economy in order to ensure the island's "survival" in a united Europe.

5. EU membership: Economic and Political Considerations

In 2004, forty years after Malta's independence, the small Mediterranean island state finally became part of a united Europe. By analysing major steps in the development of Malta-EU relations from the very beginning, starting with the Association Agreement, followed by several crises culminating in the freezing of Malta's application to political rapprochement and a pro-European referendum, it could be shown that the island's way on the road towards membership was anything but unproblematic for Malta and the EU. Smallness, insularity, neutrality, party politics and polarisation are just a few issues denoting major obstacles on Malta's journey to accession.

Since 2004, the small Mediterranean island forms part of the largest trading bloc in the world and sits at the table where far-reaching political decisions are made. In Chapter 4.5. possible alternatives to EU-membership have already been taken into consideration with the conclusion that membership seemed to be the best long-term option for the small island state. But what does it mean for Malta to be an EU member state? As already pointed out, membership does not only bring about advantages but also problems and difficulties, particularly to small countries. Hence, it is also necessary to take into account the consequences and effects of membership. Do influential economic organisations in Malta welcome or disapprove the government's membership course? Which interests does Malta pursue? Which problems or disadvantages might occur? Is the small island state able to fulfil its membership obligations? In what ways does the EU benefit from Malta's accession? These are the guiding questions in this section.

The pro-European atmosphere on the island articulated in the EU referendum and the subsequent general election indicated the Maltese government chose the right way forward. However it cannot totally be ruled out that the atmosphere may change again, especially when the negative side effects of the extensive economic reforms which have to be undertaken fully materialise. Thus, it is essential that at least some major economic actors in Malta are backing the government's position concerning membership.

The *Federation of Industries* (FOI) founded in 1946, has published several studies over the years dealing with the effects of EU membership. The overall conclusion is that although Malta's industry, especially those companies producing solely for the domestic market, have to face hard competition after accession; early industrial restructuring measures taken by the government means membership could turn out to be the right option for the small island.[172]

The Maltese *Chamber of Commerce* also seems to pursue a pro-membership attitude, especially regarding the trade opportunities with other EU-members. The *Malta Employers' Association* (MEA), founded in 1965 as a counterbalance to the powerful *General Workers' Union* (GWU), sees several difficulties and only a few advantages in membership. For example, the organisation has some doubts concerning Malta's competitiveness in a European context and thus long transitional periods would be necessary to protect Maltese companies.[173] As far as the *General Workers' Union*, Malta's largest trade union with close links to the Malta Labour Party is concerned, their position is quite clear. They have repeatedly expressed that EU-membership entails a number of disadvantages such as rising living costs and rising unemployment.[174]

Before taking a closer look at potential problematic areas linked to membership, positive effects for Malta due to EU accession shall also be taken into consideration. As far as the political sphere is concerned, through membership, Malta can improve her position in both a European and international context. The European Union is a decisive factor of regional stability not only in Europe, but also in the Mediterranean region; thus the EU, within its sphere of influence, may serve as a positive force that strengthens the conditions and chances of survival of small states like Malta.[175] Furthermore, as pointed

---

[172] Cf. Bartholy (1989), 114.

[173] Cf. Bartholy (1989), 118f.

[174] See also page 57 of this study concerning the GWU's position on the EU referendum.

[175] Cf. Pace (2001), 14.

out in the theoretical framework[176], small states often lack resources to successfully act alone in the international arena and thus acting through the EU and its policies, e.g. in the field of the *Euromed Partnership*, is possibly the best and most efficient option for a small island state like Malta.

As for the economic sphere, according to John Redmond, the EU attraction for Malta largely results from the unrestricted access to EU markets for exports and the financial assistance packages provided by the EU. Moreover, Malta may also profit from the Community's enterprise policy, as one main target of this policy is the promotion of small and medium sized enterprises (SMEs). According to the EU's definition of SMEs a vast majority of Maltese companies would fulfil these criteria and be eligible.[177]

However Ali Bayar makes clear that economic benefits due to EU membership do not happen overnight:

> "Enlargement is an unrivalled opportunity for development and growth through economies of scale, larger markets, and foreign direct investment. Industrial restructuring cannot be avoided. Delaying the necessary changes and policy measures worsen the conditions for competitiveness. Success depends on maintaining found momentum, not just on being a member of the EU. It takes time to change policies. EU membership requires concerted policy action on many different levels that take time to co-ordinate. Without strong and decisive policy measures, EU membership would not produce all its benefits. Structural policies and initiatives require years to develop and implement. It takes time for new rules and incentives to influence behaviour and investment patterns. Positive results do not materialise the day after accession." (Bayar 2003, 89)

Besides the extensive and painful restructuring of the Maltese economy, EU membership also poses various problems in the field of administration. Does Malta have enough qualified personnel, experts, specialists and administrative officers for example, to meet all membership obligations? Small states have to implement and monitor the same amount of EU rules and regulations as large states, which generally have substantial administrative machinery at

---

[176] Compare also 3.3. Small State Theory in this study.

[177] Cf. Redmond (1994), 133; Redmond (1993b), 32.

their disposal. The Maltese parliament in particular has to cope with a new and vast workload:

> "Malta's House of Representatives generally meets only three times a week for three-hour sessions in the evening enacting an average of thirty laws annually. Moreover, there are only sixty-five members of parliament and excluding the ministers and parliamentary secretaries (junior ministers) they all practise a profession or are employed on a full-time basis, so that they are in effect part-time parliamentarians. Yet this parliament must now debate and enact all the necessary legislation to align the local regime to the changing Community *acquis* and to transpose the same number of directives as the legislative bodies of larger EU countries." (Buttigieg 2004, 8)

Moreover, regarding financial means provided by the EU, for example in the field of structural policy, money is not simply transferred to eligible member states. Specific national programmes have to be set up, national co-finance has to be ensured and expenses justified; an enormous bureaucratic effort and burden for a small state. [178]

Another question which has to be raised when speaking about membership obligations is whether such a small country like Malta would be able to take over the biannually rotating Council Presidency. According to Redmond, "there must be great doubts on grounds of experience, availability of administrative and technical support and, most important, whether such a presidency would command any credibility in the rest of the world". [179]

One example of a small state which largely satisfactorily mastered this task is Luxembourg, a founding member of the EU.[180] But there is still some time to discuss this question and to take preparatory action, as Malta is scheduled to take over the Council Presidency for the first time in January 2017.[181]

Since after accession, Malta has to pay attention that her interests are not overruled in the EU decision making process:

---

[178] See also Redmond (1993a), 117.

[179] Redmond (1993a), 117f..

[180] Luxembourg, directed by Jean-Claude Juncker, took over the Council Presidency in the first half of the year 2005.

[181] <http://www.euractiv.com/en/constitution/eu-presidencies/article-138197>.

> "Community decision and policy making is on-going and unless Malta is properly represented in the decision-making bodies and its micro-state concerns adequately considered and safeguarded by a fully representative Commission, post-accession decisions could wipe out the beneficial effects that the hard earned special arrangements obtained during negotiations were intended to achieve." (Buttigieg 2004, 14)

So far in this chapter, the problems and advantages of membership have solely been analysed from a Maltese perspective. However, it is also prudent to ask how the European Union might benefit from Malta's accession. Due to Malta's small size and her limited economic influence, the accession of the island has often been described as a "side-show" for the EU, "another star on the EC flag but not much else".[182] Nevertheless, in a wider context, it becomes apparent that the Mediterranean region is of obvious political and strategic significance for the European Union, as well as of economic importance with regard to trade, tourism and oil.[183] Particularly in connection to the *Euromed Partnership* and the ambitious aim to create a *Euro-Mediterranean Free Trade Area* until 2010, often overshadowed by political crises and armed conflicts in the Middle East, the European Union's

interest in that region becomes clear. Hence, the accession of Cyprus and Malta can be seen as part of a consistent continuation of the Union's Mediterranean policy. It can also be interpreted as a positive signal to the Mediterranean states, that despite the EU's involvement in Eastern Europe, the Southern periphery of Europe has not totally been forgotten.

Although Malta's membership seems to be rather insignificant in economic terms due to the island's size, thus not causing a great financial burden for the Community, its size entails consequences in the political sphere which the EU has to deal. For example, there is the question of Malta's representation in the different EU institutions and the more general issue of how to balance the interests of the large member states with the interests of the increasing number of small states in the European Union since the last enlargement

182 Pomfret (1992), 84.

183 Cf. Redmond (1994), 133.

round.[184] As already mentioned, Malta's neutrality and the island's fast changing political attitude towards Europe in the past are further factors which might turn again into problematic issues for the European Union after Malta's accession.

[184] These issues will be dealt with in greater detail under 6. Accession Treaty and Representation in EU institutions and 7.1. Large states vs. Small states in an enlarged European Union?

6. Accession Treaty and Representation in EU institutions

The accession treaty for the 10 new member states of the fifth enlargement round of the European Union was signed on April 16 2003 in Athens by the 25 heads of state and their foreign ministers. The admission and the modalities of accession were laid down in a single document for all 10 states. The document comprises around 5,000 pages, including the comprehensive Act of Accession in which the specific conditions for membership are defined. The Act of Accession is divided into five sections. Part one deals with the main principles followed by the adjustment of the existing treaties, especially the representation of each new member state in EU institutions (part two). Part three deals with permanent provisions whereas part four is concerned with temporary provisions. Finally, in part five, provisions relating to the implementation of the act of accession can be found.[185]

The provisions concerning the representation of the new member states in EU institutions are still based on the Nice Treaty, since the ratification process of the EU constitution has been on hold due to negative referendum results in France and The Netherlands in 2005. For the legislative period 2004-2009, Malta obtained five seats in parliament, one seat less than Luxembourg or her Mediterranean partner Cyprus, although the European Parliament already recommended in 2002 that Malta, in accordance with her size, should be granted six seats in parliament.[186] Eugene Buttigieg sees a disadvantage for Malta in the allocation of only five parliamentary seats:

> "(...) the Maltese euro-parliamentarians will find it very difficult to participate effectively in the parliament's committees. The small states in the EU are actually disproportionately represented in Parliament, but this representation is still very small in order for their national interests to be adequately and effectively represented in the European Parliament." (Buttigieg 2004, 10)

---

[185] Cf. Lippert (2004), 47-49.

[186] Cf. European Parliament: Report on Enlargement, 19.

The situation may improve for Malta in the near future, as in the EU constitution a minimum number of six parliamentarians is stipulated from 2009 onwards. This provision will only materialise if the EU Constitution comes into force.

Like other member states, Malta is appointed the same number of representatives in the Commission and the European Court of Justice. In the Council, Malta, as the smallest member state, has three votes compared to four for Cyprus and Luxembourg. Sieglinde Gstöhl observes in this context that despite Luxembourg's and Malta's comparable demographic size, (Luxembourg has a population of around 470,000 and Malta close to 400,000) there seems to exist a kind of invisible divide between the two smallest member states of the European Union, possibly a result of Luxembourg's status as a founding EU member.[187] Thus, one consequence could be that "for Malta's voice to be heard it has to rely even more on forging alliances with other States than larger States that require fewer allies for a blocking minority".[188]

[187] Cf. Gstöhl (2001), 121.

[188] Buttigieg (2004), 11.

7. Malta in the EU: Issue of Smallness & Political Priorities

Malta's way into the European Union has been detailed in depth by explaining major events and developments, and by paying attention to specific problems, advantages, political considerations and the question of representation in EU institutions. It is now time to focus on the present and maybe even the future by taking a closer look at Malta's position within the EU. Do the small island state's membership expectations concerning a gain in prosperity, influence, power and security materialise? Is the small Mediterranean island state able to defend its interest and to put through its priority agendas in concert with 24 larger member states? What are Malta's priority issues and political concerns in a European context? Is there a power-related division between large and smaller member states in the EU? These are the guiding questions for the analysis in this chapter.

7.1. Large states versus small states in an Enlarged Union?

After having outlined the position of small states in the international system from a theoretical perspective in chapter 3.3., the focus in this subchapter will be exclusively on the position and the status of small states within the European Union.

A predestined function for small states in the EU is, as Zibrandt in his study focusing on Belgium, Luxembourg, the Netherlands, Ireland and Denmark observes, that of a "service state". These small states tend to see themselves as states whose role it is to serve as bridge-builders and mediators between certain member states, or to function as host countries for EU institutions or conferences:

> "Die fünf Kleinstaaten sehen sich gerne als Brückenbauer zu anderen Ländern, als Vermittler oder Mediatoren in Verhandlungen, als Kenner bestimmter Staaten oder Spezialisten für besondere Fragen und als Gastgeberländer für EG-Institutionen. Durch diese Dienstleistungen gegenüber der Gemeinschaft versuche sie, sich Goodwill zu verschaffen. Die Anwendung

> dieser Strategien verleiht den Kleinstaaten das Image von Servicestaaten." (Zibrandt von Dosenrode-Lynge 1993, 407)

Concerning the categorisation of small states in the EU, the already mentioned lack of a universal definition also exists in a European context. In the chapter on small state theory it was shown that there exists no consensus about how to define a "small state".[189] Therefore, it is unsurprising that even the European Union has no explicit definition. It can be assumed, however, that the EU utilises the criterion "population" as demarcation for smallness, for example the number of votes in the Council for each member state is distributed according to population.[190] Nevertheless, in the literature there exists slight differences in classifying the member states of the European Union into the category of large and small states. Regarding the EU composed of 27 members, Thomas Jansen speaks of 7 EU members belonging to the category of large states and 20 countries belonging to the category of small states.[191] Neill Nugent draws a similar dividing line by stating that 19 of the 27 members will have a population of less than 12 million.[192] The former chairman of the European Convention Valery Giscard d'Estaing proposes a division into three categories for the member states of the EU-25:

> "(...) the EU now comprises three categories of states: the six largest ones, with a population of more than fourty [*sic* forty] million inhabitants, which, together, amount to 74% of the EU population; eight medium-sized countries, with a population between 8 and 16 million people, who represent 19% of the population; and eleven small states who, together, only include 7% of the population." (Giscard d'Estaing, cited in Magnette/ Nicolaïdis [n.d.], 24)

Whatever the exact classification of EU member states with populations ranging between 400,000 and 82 million might look like, the important question is are there colliding interests and different attitudes arising from this variation in size? Already in the 1980s Mario Hirsch, who analysed the case of Luxem-

---

[189] Cf. 3.3.1. Difficulties in defining "smallness".

[190] Cf. Gstöhl (2001), 103.

[191] Jansen (2001), 176. The European Union with 27 member states already includes Romania and Bulgaria, two candidate countries which will join the EU in 2007.

[192] See Nugent (2003), 503.

bourg, argued that "the EEC is not the safeguard which shields a small member state from economic setbacks, nor does it put the small state on a par with the larger members". He goes on stating that "the right to invoke a national interest is increasingly denied to the small state, especially if such interests collide with those of more powerful countries".[193]

The European Union finally had to deal with the question of small states when in the 1990s numerous smaller and middle-sized countries applied for membership. It became clear that the existing institutional structures originally set up for the six founding members would be overstrained in the near future and needed to be revised. In a document published by the European Commission in 1992 entitled *Europe and the challenge of enlargement* the Commission, taking Cyprus and Malta as an example, pointed out that

> "in the case of Malta and Cyprus, the adoption of the Community *acquis* would appear to pose no insuperable problems. However, both are very small States, and the question of their participation in the Community institutions would have to be resolved in an appropriate manner in accession negotiations".[194]

One decree of the EU has been the equality of member states irrespective their size. This is, for example, expressed in the fact that every member state nominates one Commissioner, and that smaller member states take their turn in the rotating Council Presidency. However, in an enlarged European Union the preservation of equality has become an even more difficult task. This does not automatically mean that only the larger member states may profit from this situation. As far as the seats in the European Parliament are concerned, small states are clearly over-represented compared to their population. Thus, especially after the enlargement round of 2004, some larger EU member states fear a gradual loss of power:

> "But the prospect of enlargement to East and Central Europe which was to bring membership from 15 to 27 and eventually more was bound to exaggerate the tensions between the two principles of proportional representation and equality between states. Unsurprisingly, the big countries in-

---

[193] Hirsch (1983), 130.

[194] Europe and the Challenge of Enlargement, 24 June 1992, 17f.

> creasingly fell prey to what some referred to as the "Lilliput syndrome," picturing themselves as the giants potentially held back by a crowd of mini countries." (Magnette/ Nicolaidïs [n.d.], 8)

Magnette and Nicolaidïs go on stating that supranational institutions are supposed to disproportionately serve weaker, i.e. generally smaller, actors.[195]

Considering the different EU institutions, it is plausible that small states tend to regard the Commission as the major advocate of their interests, whereas the larger states see the Council as their main agency to exert influence and to put through their specific interests:

> "Over time, the smaller member states have come to see the Commission as the best institutional protection of their interests, with its propensity to use the monopoly of initiative to fulfill its mission as guardian of the treaty and counterbalance the big states. As the Commission generally proved to be truly independent and driven by European interests, the Benelux countries became its most loyal supporters. So did the other small and medium countries who came to join the Union." (Magnette/ Nicolaidïs [n.d.], 6)

These statements seem to indicate that the small states' interests are largely identical and that smaller EU countries work together in order to stand up to the larger states. In practice, such behaviour is rarely the case. There actually exists a high degree of heterogeneity between the smaller EU members as far as interests are concerned, so that purely small state coalitions hardly ever come about.[196]

An instance where small state coalitions are likely and alliances formed among small EU states, is when treaties are amended or modified, especially when the institutional structure and the balance of power are concerned. In other words: "but as soon as institutional matters are on the table, the smaller member states tend to unite".[197]

The most recent situation of this kind were debates about European Constitution drafting. From a theoretical perspective, the Constitution in general

---

[195] Magnette/ Nicolaidïs [n.d.], 6.

[196] See also Magnette/ Nicolaidïs [n.d.], 3.

[197] Magnette/ Nicolaidïs [n.d.], 3.

would not have a negative effect on the position of small EU states, maybe even improving the small states' status:

> "From the standpoint of small state theory, a European constitution (...) has important implications. (...), in international relations small states prefer that inter-state relations be regulated by international law because their rights can better be safeguarded than in an anarchical world where relations are based on power. The European Union, (...), reduces the anarchical nature of the system. It clarifies the 'rules of the game' by which small and large states alike operate within it, thus providing a more stable inter-state system of relations." (Pace 2001, 96)

As far as Malta in particular and the EU Constitution is concerned, Peter G. Xuereb, Jean Monnet Professor in EU Law and European Integration at the University of Malta, concluded in his article on *The Draft Treaty establishing a Constitution for Europe – What it means for us*:

> "I support, indeed welcome, the Constitutional treaty. Broad reason: *It is a clear improvement* in terms of loyalty and fairness as between Member States and citizens of the Union; in terms of democracy and openness in decision-making at European level; and in terms of capacity, promised effecttiveness and efficiency in tackling common challenges and threats including those external threats we all face and face better together." (Xuereb [n.d.], 5)

A definite answer concerning the effects of the EU Constitution on the (power) balance between large and small member states can only be given if or when the ratification process is resumed, and the EU Constitution finally comes into force.

The conclusion which can be drawn from the above analysis is that although small states tend to unite in special cases while large states take advantage of their size and influence in EU institutions, even against the interests of smaller states, it cannot be said that there exists a clear-cut small state and large state "camp" within the European Union.

7.2. Malta's Priority Agendas as EU Member

Malta's policy agendas before 2004 were largely directed towards EU accession, e.g. establishing good relations with the European Union, setting up the necessary national institutional structures, trying to meet the Copenhagen Criteria and trying to prepare Malta's economy for membership. Post-accession, the Maltese government is in a position to modify its main priorities and to extend the scope of policy issues. One the one hand, EU membership offers new ways of governance for the small Mediterranean island state and is likely to strengthen Malta's position in negotiations with third countries. On the other hand, the Maltese government has to make sure major national interests do not get lost in the massive "EU machinery," and that Malta's concerns regarding specific policy fields are adequately taken into account by other member states and by the EU institutions.

Consequently, the guiding question for this subchapter is: What are Malta's policy priorities as an EU member state? Since Malta is active in numerous political fields, only the most current topics and those with a particular relevance for Malta in a European context have been selected and will be analysed in this section. For structural purposes, a division into foreign and domestic policy agendas will be made, although some of the issues which will be discussed affect more than one political sphere.

7.2.1. Foreign Policy Agenda

A document published by the Maltese *External Affairs Directorate* outlines Malta's foreign policy priorities from a geopolitical perspective. They include, among others, the Middle East Peace Process, relations with Libya, Tunisia and Egypt, the European Neighbourhood Policy, the EU's Strategic Partnership with Mediterranean countries and the Middle East and the issue of illegal immigration.[198] It is by no means surprising that Malta's foreign policy agenda is almost exclusively focused on the Mediterranean region. As already argued in the chapter on small states' foreign policy

---

[198] External Affairs Directorate, Malta. http://www.foreign.gov.mt/pages.aspx?page=48.

behaviour, small states do not have enough human and material resources to exercise an all-embracing foreign policy; thus tending to concentrate on neighbouring regions and specific issues such as potential security threats.[199]

The above mentioned priorities are all linked in one way or another, to the so-called *Euro-Mediterranean Partnership*, which was recently incorporated into the framework of the *European Neighbourhood Policy* (ENP). The Euromed Partnership launched in 1995, constitutes the general framework for the relations between the European Union and the countries in the south and east of the Mediterranean area.[200] The main objective of the Euromed Partnership has been and still is to achieve "a common area of peace, stability and prosperity in the Mediterranean region".[201] One concrete project is the establishment of a free trade area across the Mediterranean region by 2010. Many critics argue little progress has been made since the launch of the Euromed Partnership in 1995. Some observers hope that under the new framework of the European Neighbourhood Policy, due to its bilateral and more differentiated approach, the Euromed Partnership might finally turn into a success.[202]

The Maltese government backs the ENP initiative:

> Malta welcomed the launching of the European Neighbourhood Policy (ENP) as a new framework for relations with all the EU's neighbours in order to reduce the risks of instability in its periphery. (...) Malta considers the ENP as providing an opportunity to build upon the 'horizontal' Barcelona Process by reviewing and enhancing 'vertical' cooperation between the Euro-Mediterranean Partners. (...) The ENP provides Malta with an opportunity to contribute in areas of primary interest, such as management of migration flows, promotion of human rights, democratisation, counter-proliferation and coun-

---

[199] See also 3.3.3. Small states' foreign policy behaviour in this study.

[200] This means that there are 35 countries involved in this process (EU-25, Algeria, Egypt, Israel, Jordan, Lebanon, Morocco, Palestine, Syria, Tunisia, Turkey). Libya has observer status since 1999. Cf. http://ec.europa.eu/comm/external_relations/euromed/index.htm.

[201] Chairman's Statement 10th Anniversary Euro-Mediterranean Summit. http://ec.europa.eu/comm/external_relations/euromed/summit1105/chairmans_statement.pdf

[202] Cf. Stratenschulte [n.d.], 2.

> ter-terrorism efforts, and the acceleration of increased market integration with the objective of improving the investment climate in the region.[203]

Malta has the advantage of being familiar with “both sides”. Before membership, Malta belonged to the group of associated Mediterranean partners for a number of years. Now, as a member of the European Union, Malta’s aim is to actively promote the Euromed Partnership. Due to Malta’s well-established bilateral relations with Libya, she would welcome seeing her Mediterranean neighbour become a full member of the initiative. Promoting the Euromed Parterhip is a very ambitious task, as Mediterranean countries from the southern littoral form a highly heterogeneous group. Above all, the region is marked by instability, rapid change and political crises culminating in armed conflicts such as that between Lebanon and Israel. It is a well-known fact that Malta alone does not have the means and the resources to play a leading role in the Euro-Mediterranean Partnership, but the small island could definitely make valuable contributions by acting as a messenger, intermediary, initiator of third solutions or as a provider of constructive impulse in times of stalemate by making use of its position as an island state belonging to both regions.[204]

Another issue which ranks high on Malta’s foreign policy agenda at present is the issue of illegal immigration. Since membership, Malta is the southernmost tip of the European Union and especially affected by continuing waves of illegal immigrants from Africa.[205] The Maltese government has repeatedly asked the European Union for help. It rightly argues that illegal immigration does not only pose a problem to Malta, but it concerns the whole Mediterranean region, thus the European Union has to deal with this matter. In a statement by the Minister of Foreign Affairs, Dr Michael Frendo, to EU Ambassadors in Malta, Dr Frendo points out that “since 20 June, Malta has witnessed the arrival of over 500 illegal immigrants from North Africa. This amount brings the

---

[203] External Affairs Directorate, Malta. http://www.foreign.gov.mt/pages.aspx?page=48

[204] Compare also Pace (2000), 7; Pace (2001), 406.

[205] Cf. Ministry of Foreign Affairs, Malta. Speaking Notes on Illegal Immigration to Malta, 5th July 2005.

number of illegal immigrants arriving in Malta since January 2006 to 967".[206] This number does not appear high compared to other illegal immigration flows to Spain or to Italy. But for a tiny island already densely populated, such a number of immigrants in a short period of time stretches the island's humanitarian capacities beyond its limits and poses a serious problem to the Maltese government. In this difficult situation, the Maltese Foreign Minister expresses his discontent about the Union's lack of commitment by alluding to the issue of smallness: "The European Union is dealing with Malta with the mentality of 'small countries, small problems' and this is unacceptable". He goes on stating that "all attention is on Spain which is getting assistance and Malta is being left in the lurch".[207] The European Union reacted by putting the topic of illegal immigration as the main item on the General Affairs agenda of the EU Foreign Minister's Council meeting on July 17th 2006. Measures undertaken in order to mitigate the situation in Malta are the launch of the EU's joint patrols in the Mediterranean and the proposal by the Commission to consider dispatching teams of border guards, interpreters and medics to help frontline states such as Malta to cope with the number of illegal immigrants.[208] It still remains to be seen whether these measures produce the desired results. What can already be stated in this respect is that persistence of the small Mediterranean island succeeded in focusing the EU's attention on a priority agenda of the Maltese government.

7.2.2. Domestic Priorities

In the field of domestic policies one main priority was and still is to boost the Maltese economy with the right policy measures by simultaneously consolidating public finances. The consolidation of public finances is of particular importance as the Maltese government plans to join the Euro Zone in 2008. Before adopting the Euro, the new member states must fulfil the convergence

---

[206] Statement by the Minister of Foreign Affairs Dr. Michael Frendo, press release 4th July 2006: Foreign Minister raises illegal immigration with resident EU Ambassadors.

[207] Press Release Ministry of Foreign Affairs, Malta, 30th June 2006: EU lacks real commitment for Malta's illegal immigration problem.

[208] Cf. Stephen Calleya, Migration in the Euro-Med area. Times of Malta, 26th July, 2006.

criteria, e.g. an annual government deficit to GDP below 3% and a gross government debt to GDP below 60%.

In a strategy paper published by the Maltese government and the Central Bank of Malta, it is declared that the Maltese economy is in principal ready to join the Euro Zone:

> "The Maltese economy is well suited to participate in the EU single currency area. It is small and open and is already closely integrated with the EU economy; it also has similarities with the euro area in the sectoral composition of employment and GDP and in financial sector integration, as well as a relatively high degree of business cycle synchronization; and the currency is strongly pegged to the euro. These factors should serve to mitigate the degree of vulnerability to asymmetric shocks".[209]

But the Maltese government also admits that the fulfilment of some of the convergence criteria poses a major problem for the small island state:

> "The major challenge to Malta's full compliance with the nominal convergence criteria is the fulfilment of the fiscal conditions. This is because the other Maastricht criteria relating to the long-term interest rate and, to a lesser extent, to inflation appear to be achievable and there are no unequivocal indications of significant misalignment in the value of the Maltese lira. The fiscal deficit, in contrast, is well above the 3% of GDP reference value set out by the Treaty, while the public debt/GDP ratio, which is the other fiscal criterion, also exceeds the reference value of 60%."[210]

In order to tackle this problem, the government implemented a *Convergence Programme*. One objective of this programme is to reduce the fiscal deficit from 5.2% in 2004 to 1.4% in 2007.[211] Furthermore, a *National Euro Changeover Committee* (NECC) was set up to guarantee a smooth transition from the Maltese lira to the Euro and to inform the public about the coming changes.[212] Malta anticipates that the Maltese economy profits from the change-

---

[209] Government of Malta / Central Bank of Malta. Malta's strategy for participating in economic and monetary union and adopting the Euro, 6.

[210] Government of Malta / Central Bank of Malta. Malta's strategy for participating in economic and monetary union and adopting the Euro, 6f.

[211] Cf. Government of Malta / Central Bank of Malta. Malta's strategy for participating in economic and monetary union and adopting the Euro, 27.

[212] For more information about NECC see also <http://euro.gov.mt>.

over in the long run, as Prime Minister Lawrence Gonzi points out: "Upon adoption of the Euro we expect to reap gains from the elimination of exchange rate risk and reduced transaction costs across most of our external transactions".[213] The European currency could thus also be helpful to attract more foreign direct investments to Malta, which would be beneficial to the Maltese economy.

This exemplary analysis of specific policy priorities of the Maltese government has shown that as a fully-fledged member of the European Union, Malta is now in a position to deal with a wider scope of policy issues and to extend her presence not only in Europe, but also in the international arena. On the flipside there are new problems and challenges arising from EU membership, namely the influx of illegal immigrants and the heavy economic restructuring necessary to reach a sustainable level of competitiveness in the European Union.

---

[213] Speech by the prime minister, 2nd June 2006.

8. Conclusion

The aim of this paper was to provide a comprehensive picture of Malta's way into the European Union by analysing the island's relationship with the EU from the beginning up to now. Decisive factors such as smallness, insularity, and vulnerability were presented and their effects on a state's behaviour were examined by taking the small Mediterranean island state Malta as an example.

In the first part of the study, a comprehensive theoretical framework was established as the basis for systematic analyses. Due to the complexity of the topic, several theoretical approaches from international relations and European Integration have been taken into consideration to create a complex picture about the theoretical findings on small states and integration.

In the field of European Integration theory, two influential approaches neo-functionalism and liberal intergovernmentalism have been scrutinised with the aim to extract suitable categories and variables concerning Malta-EU relations. The focus of neo-functionalism is on the inner dynamics of the integration process and on the role of supranational actors in this process. From a neo-functionalist point of view, the last enlargement round of the European Union including Malta can be explained as a "geographical spill-over" to strengthen the cohesion and the sphere of influence of the EU. In contrast to that, the state-centric model of intergovernmentalism considers the states as the main actors in the international arena who rationally calculate the opportunities and costs of integrating new members into the European Union.

In the next step, theoretical findings concerning a state's foreign policy behaviour were taken into closer consideration. The most prominent approaches in this field are neorealism, utilitarian liberalism and constructivism. It was pointed out that neorealism perceives the international system as being anarchic with changing power structures which may easily lead to a so-called "security dilemma" for the states. According to the neorealist approach, preserving and extending autonomy and influence are a state's main priorities in order to maintain security. For neorealists, state cooperation and the integration of states in supranational organisations are rather destructive as they entail a loss of autonomy and no real gain in influence.

In utilitarian liberalism, it is not the states, but individuals and societal groups who are in the focus of attention. It is argued that they, due to their domestic interests, determine a state's foreign policy behaviour. Despite its coherent argumentation, this approach turned out to be only partly applicable in the context of Malta-EU relations.

The third approach, namely the norm-based concept of constructivism, was rejected as underlying theoretical approach for further analysis. The reasons are that the expectations of behaviour addressed by international institutions or by domestic society cannot clearly be separated and that by applying the constructivist approach, there exists the danger of retrospectively explaining social behaviour.

Small state theory has constituted the third theoretical component in this study. This often neglected and highly diversified approach turned out to be a valuable theoretical tool in analysing Malta-EU relations. The main dispute between scholars of small state research concerns the definition of the term "small state". Various classifications have been proposed, taking into account factors such as population, GDP and size. Another approach suggested by Robert O. Keohane, classifies states according to their systemic role in international politics. It has been argued that Malta may best be described as *system-ineffectual state*, meaning that Malta is not able to influence the system alone, but rather adjusts to reality than actively shaping it. However, through EU membership Malta was able to enhance its status in international politics and can now, according to this schema, be classified as *system-affecting* state.[214] In a second step, problems and difficulties of small states have been outlined and analysed. Vulnerability in political and economic terms is a major factor in this context. Economically, small states face a number of disadvantages, such as a less diversified economic structure, limited raw materials

[214] Compare also page 22-23 in this study.

and natural resources, a small domestic market causing a limited ability to exploit economies of scale, heavy dependence on foreign trade and lack of qualified human resources.[215]

Concerning a small state's foreign policy behaviour features such as low level of participation in world affairs, addressing a narrow scope of foreign policy issues, focusing on neighbouring geographic areas and joining international institutions have been identified. It was shown that they largely apply to the small Mediterranean island state of Malta.

Following the establishment of a theoretical framework, major stages of Malta-EU relations have been analysed by applying a political approach and by paying special attention to the particularities of Malta's party system and to its close relationship with its Mediterranean neighbours. Several set backs and a struggle to find and maintain its position in Europe against various restraints, mark the forty year history of Malta-EU relations.

In the first phase of Malta-EU relations, the Association Agreement with the European Union helped Malta reduce her economic dependence on Great Britain, and to strengthen her position as a young, independent nation. From a political perspective, a change in government on the island shortly after the signing of the Association Agreement, entailed a change in Malta's foreign policy away from Europe and towards a policy of mixed alliances. Attention was drawn to the fact that political leaders with their individual opinions exert far-reaching influence on the small island's policy agenda. This phenomenon is closely linked to the distinctive Maltese political culture and de facto two party system. Main characteristics of the island's extraordinary political system are high degrees of polarisation, personalisation, mobilisation of potential voters and patron-client relationships resulting in very high turnouts of voters. The country's political division is enforced by the parties' conflicting positions on European integration. The Nationalist Party has stressed its pro-European attitude throughout the decades. The Malta Labour Party however saw more threats than benefits in EU-membership, and expressed its fears and con-

[215] Cf. Streeten (1993), 197f. Cf. also Briguglio (1995), 1616.

cerns in ambiguous and provocative foreign policy attitudes which repeatedly led to tensions between Malta and the European Union; ultimately prolonging Malta's way into the European Union. Despite these obstacles and delays, the pro-European Nationalist Party finally applied for EU membership in 1990 and the direction was clear:

> "Malta's place is in a united Europe. Economics dictate it. Politically we have to find a way of achieving it." (Pace 1990, 15)

Even the freezing of Malta's application initiated by the Euro-sceptic Malta Labour Party in 1996 only interrupted Malta's accession process for a short period.

Forty years of Malta-EU relations finally culminated in Malta's accession in 2004. The small Mediterranean island state has found its place in a united Europe. Through its efforts, Malta has attained her goal, though has no time to rest and reap the benefits of membership. As the smallest pillar of the "fortress Europe", Malta's main priority will be to defend and enforce her own interests and to make herself heard in this powerful organisation while trying to fulfil its membership obligations. This might turn out to be a very challenging task when considering Malta's scarce resources. From today's point of view, it seems to be unquestionable that EU membership was the right option for Malta. It remains to be seen if the small island can exploit all the possibilities the EU has to offer, and if she can present herself as an essential and dutiful part of this powerful community.

References

Abt, Clark C./ Deutsch, Karl W. (1993). "Basic Problems of Small Countries". In: Waschkuhn, Arno (ed.). Kleinstaat: Grundsätzliche und aktuelle Probleme. Vaduz: Verlag der Liechtensteinischen Akademischen Gesellschaft, 19-30.

Armstrong, Harvey/ Read, Robert (1995). "Western European Micro-States and EU Autonomous Regions: The Advantages of Size and Sovereignty". In: World Development Volume 23, No. 7, 1229-1245.

Axt, Heinz-Jürgen (2003). „Malta". In: Weidenfeld, Werner/ Wessels, Wolfgang (eds.). Jahrbuch der Europäischen Integration 2002/2003. Bonn: Europa Union Verlag, 441-442.

Ayres, Ron (1997). "Trade and European Integration: Malta and Cyprus 1987-1994". In: Bank of Valletta Review, No. 15, 1-32.

Baker Fox, Annette (1959). The Power of Small States. Diplomacy in World War II. Chicago: University of Chicago Press,

Baldacchino, Godfrey (2002). "Malta, National Identity and the EU". In: West European Politics. Volume 25, No. 4, 191-206.

Bartholy, Heike (1989). Malta und die Europäische Gemeinschaft: Sozioökonomische Aspekte eines EG-Beitritts. Augsburg : Lehrstuhl für Soziologie u. Kommunikationswiss. d. Univ. Augsburg

Baumann, Rainer/ Rittberger, Volker/ Wagner, Wolfgang (2000). Power and Power Politics: Neorealist Foreign Policy Theory and Expectations about German Foreign Policy since Unification. http://w210.ub.uni-tuebingen.de/dbt/volltexte/2000/147/ (28.04.2006)

Bauwens, Werner/ Clesse, Armand/ Knudsen, Olav F. (eds.), 1996. Small States and the Security Challenge in the New Europe. London: Brassey's.

Bayar, Ali. (2003). Malta and the EU: Membership and Non-Membership. The Costs and Benefits. Valletta <http://www.targetltd.com/grtu> (04.04.2006)

Bestler, Anita/ Waschkuhn, Arno (2003). „Das politische System Maltas". In: Ismayr, Wolfgang (ed.). Die politischen Systeme Westeuropas. Opladen: Leske & Budrich Verlag, 731-757.

Bestler, Anita (2005). "Malta: Political Polarization on EU-Membership". In: Hrbek, Rudolf (ed.) European Parliament Elections 2004 in the 10 New Member States – Towards the Future European Party System. Baden-Baden: Nomos Verlagsgesellschaft.

Bhuglah, Assad/ Briguglio, Lino/ Witter, Michael [n.d.]. Measuring and Managing the Economic Vulnerability of Small Island Developing States. <http://www.undp.org/bpoa+10/ docs/EconomicVulnerability.pdf> (04.05.2006)

Bienen, Derk/ Freund, Corinna/ Rittberger, Volker (2000). Societal Interests, Policy Networks and Foreign Policy: An Outline of Utilitarian-Liberal Foreign Policy Theory. <http://w210.ub.uni-tuebingen.de/dbt/volltexte/2000/143/> (28.04.2006)

Boekle, Henning/ Rittberger, Volker/ Wagner, Wolfgang (2000). Norms and Foreign Policy: Constructivist Foreign Policy Theory. <http://w210.ub.uni-tuebingen.de/dbt/volltexte/2000/ 136/ (27.04.2006)

Borda, Manuel (1997). "Small Country Size and Economic Performance". In: Bank of Valletta Review, No. 16, 11-28.

Borg, Saviour F. (1993). "International Initiatives taken by the Maltese Government with regard to Islands and Small States". In: Bank of Valletta Review, No. 7, 63-79.

Briguglio, Lino (1995). "Small Island Developing States and Their Economic Vulnerabilities". In: World Development, Volume 23, No. 9, 1615-1632.

Buttigieg, Eugene (2004). Challenges Facing Malta As A Micro-State In An Enlarged EU. Bank of Valletta Review, No. 29, <http://www.bov.com/pdf/bov_ review 29-1.pdf> (04.04.2006)

Calleya, Stephen (2000). EU enlargement: the case of Malta. Challenge Europe Issue 2 - EU Enlargement: A Tryst with History, <http://www.theepc.be/en/ce.asp?TYP=CE&LV =177 &see=y&t=42&PG=CE/EN/detail&l=13&AI=37> (05.07.2006)

Calleya, Stephen (2006). Migration in the Euro-Med area. Times of Malta, July 26th <http://www.timesofmalta.com/core/article.php?id=231932> (31.07.2006)

Christmas-Møller, Wilhelm (1983). „Some Thoughts on the Scientific Applicability of the Small State Concept: A Research History and a Discussion". In: Höll, Otmar (ed.). Small States in Europe and Dependence. Wien: Wilhelm Braumüller Universitäts-Verlagsbuchandlung, 35-53.

Cini, Michelle (2003a). Referendum Briefing No 2 The Maltese EU Accession Referendum of 8 March 2003. <http://www.sussex.ac.uk/sei/documents/maltese2.pdf> (31.03.2006).

Cini, Michelle (2003b). The Maltese Parliamentary Elections of April 2003. <http://www.sussex.ac.uk/sei/documents/oernmaltabp12.pdf> (31.03.2006).

Cini, Michelle (2004). "Culture, Institutions and Campaign Effects: Explaining the Outcome of Malta's EU Accession Referendum". In: Western European Politics Volume 27, No. 4, [Special Issue on: Choosing Union: The 2003 EU Accession Referendums, ed. by Szczerbiak, Aleks/ Taggart, Paul], 584-602.

Clarke, Colin/ Payne, Tony (eds.) 1987. Politics, Security and Development in Small States. London: Allen & Unwin.

Craig, James (1987). "Malta". In: Clarke, Colin/ Payne, Tony (eds.). Politics, Security and Development in Small States. London: Allen & Unwin, 170-183.

Eisenstadt, Shmuel Noah (1993). "Small States in the 'Post-Modern' Era". In: Waschkuhn, Arno (ed.). Kleinstaat: Grundsätzliche und aktuelle Probleme. Vaduz: Verlag der Liechtensteinischen Akademischen Gesellschaft, 107-117.

Espíndola, Roberto (1987). "Security Dilemmas". In: Clarke, Colin/ Payne, Tony (eds.). Politics, Security and Development in Small States. London: Allen & Unwin, 63-79.

Federation of Industries, Malta (1988). The EC: Malta at the crossroads: Evaluating the effects of the island's future relations with the European Community.

Fenech, Dominic (1988). "The 1987 Maltese Election: Between Europe and the Mediterranean". In: West European Politics, Volume 11, No. 1, 133-138.

Geser, Hans (2001). "Was ist eigentlich ein Kleinstaat?" In: Kirt, Romain/ Waschkuhn, Arno (eds.). Kleinstaaten-Kontinent Europa: Probleme und Perspektiven. Baden-Baden: Nomos Verlagsgesellschaft, 89-100.

Gstöhl, Sieglinde (2001). "Der Mikrostaat als Variante des Kleinstaats? Erfahrungen mit UNO und EU". In: Kirt, Romain/ Waschkuhn, Arno (ed.). Kleinstaaten-Kontinent Europa: Probleme und Perspektiven. Baden-Baden: Nomos Verlagsgesellschaft, 101-124.

Hall, Derek (ed.) 2000. Europe goes east: EU enlargement, diversity and uncertainty. London: Stationery Office.

Hey, Jeanne A.K. (2003). Small States in World Politics: Explaining Foreign Policy Behavior. London: Lynne Rienner Publishers.

Hirczy, Wolfgang (1995). "Explaining near-universal turnout: The Case of Malta". In: European Journal of Political Research, Volume 27, 255-272.

Hirsch, Mario (1983). "Who is in Charge of the Destinies of Small States? The Case of Luxemburg." In: Höll, Otmar (ed.). Small States in Europe and Dependence. Wien: Wilhelm Braumüller Universitäts-Verlagsbuchhandlung, 130-139.

Holsti, K.J. (1970), "National Role Conceptions in the Study of Foreign Policy". In: International Studies Quarterly. Vol. 14, No. 3, 233-309.

Höll, Otmar (ed.) 1983. Small States in Europe and Dependence. Wien: Wilhelm Braumüller Universitäts-Verlagsbuchhandlung.

Jansen, Thomas (2001). "Zur Außenpolitik kleiner Staaten". In: Kirt, Romain/ Waschkuhn, Arno (eds.). Kleinstaaten-Kontinent Europa: Probleme und Perspektiven. Baden-Baden: Nomos Verlagsgesellschaft, 169-180.

Khalaf, Nadim G. (1971). Economic Implications of the Size of Nations with Special Reference to Lebanon. Leiden: E. J. Brill.

Kirt, Romain/ Waschkuhn, Arno (eds.) 2001. Kleinstaaten-Kontinent Europa: Probleme und Perspektiven. Baden-Baden: Nomos Verlagsgesellschaft.

Knodt, Michèle/ Große Hüttmann, Martin (2005). Der Multi-Level Governance-Ansatz. In: Bieling, Hans-Jürgen/ Lerch, Marika (eds.). Theorien der europäischen Integration. Wiesbaden: Verlag für Sozialwissenschaften, 223-247.

Koßdorff, Felix (2000). Die Republik Irland: ein europäischer Kleinstaat und seine außenpolitischen Strategien als Mitglied der EU. Wien: WUV.

Kramer, Helmut (1993). "Kleinstaaten-Theorie und Kleinstaaten-Aussenpolitik in Europa". In: Waschkuhn, Arno (ed.). Kleinstaat: Grundsätzliche und aktuelle Probleme. Vaduz: Verlag der Liechtensteinischen Akademischen Gesellschaft, 247-259.

Kreile, Michael (2004). „Die Osterweiterung der Europäischen Union". In: Weidenfeld, Werner (ed.). Die Europäische Union: Politisches System und Politikbereiche. Band 442. Bonn: bpb, 50-672.

Landaburu Illarramendi, E. (1994). "The EU Regional Policy and the Maltese Islands". Bank of Valletta Review, No. 10, 1-14.

Laursen, Finn [n.d.]. Theories of European Integration. <http://www.lib.tku. edu.tw/ libeu/eulecture/Theories%20of%20European%20Integration.pdf> (24.04.2006)

Lindberg, Leon N. (1963). The Political Dynamics of European Economic Integration. Stanford: Stanford University Press.

Lippert, Barbara (2003). „Erweiterungspolitik der Europäischen Union". In: Weidenfeld, Werner/ Wessels, Wolfgang (eds.), Jahrbuch der Europäischen Integration 2002/ 2003. Bonn: Europa Union Verlag, 417-430.

Lippert, Barbara (2004). „Glanzloser Arbeitserfolg von epochaler Bedeutung: eine Bilanz der EU-Erweiterungspolitik 1989-2004". In: Lippert, Barbara (ed.). Bilanz und Folgeprobleme der EU-Erweiterung. Baden-Baden: Nomos Verlagsgesellschaft, 13-71.

Lowenthal, David (1987). "Social Features". In: Clarke, Colin/ Payne, Tony (eds.). Politics, Security and Development in Small States. London: Allen & Unwin, 27-49.

Magnette, Paul/ Nicolaïdis, Kalypso [n.d.]. Large and Small Member States in the European Union: Reinventing the Balance. <http://www.notre-europe.asso.fr/ Etud25-fr> (03.05.2006)

Magnússon, Magnús Árni [n.d.]. Culture, economics and security in the debate on European integration in Iceland and Malta. Working paper. (Received author's permission to quote from this paper). <http://www.bifrost.is/Files/Skra_0003005.pdf> (11.04.2006)

Marks, Gary/ Hooghe, Lisbet (2004). Multi-Level Governance and European Integration. Lanham: Rowman and Littlefield.

Ministry for Economic Services (2003). Prosperity In Change The Way Forward: National Industrial Policy. Malta.

Mouritzen, Hans A. (1983). "Defensive Acquiescence: Making the Best out of Dependence". In: Höll, Otmar (ed.). Small States in Europe and Dependence. Wien: Wilhelm Braumüller Universitäts-Verlagsbuchhandlung, 239-261.

Nugent, Neill (2003). The Government and Politics of the European Union. New York: Palgrave.

Pace, Roderick (1990). "Malta's EC Application: Some Economic and Political Considerations". In: Bank of Valletta Review, No. 1, 1-15.

Pace, Roderick (1997). The European Union's next Mediterranean Enlargement. Jean Monnet Working Papers in Comparative and International Politics. <http://www.fscpo.unict.it/EuroMed/jmwp06.htm> (23.03.2006)

Pace, Roderick (2000). The Accession of Cyprus and Malta in the European Union and Its Effect on the Euro-Mediterranean Partnership. <http://www.ecsanet. org/fifth_ecsaworld/index.htm> (30.03.2006).

Pace, Roderick (2001). Microstate Security in the Global System: EU-Malta Relations. Midsea Books.

Pace, Roderick (2002). "A Small State and the European Union: Malta's EU Accession Experience." In: South European Society & Politics, Vol. 7, No.1.

Pace, Roderick (2004). European Parliament Election Briefing No 5. The European Parliament Election in Malta June 12, 2004. <http://www.sussex.ac.uk/sei/documents/epernep2004malta.pdf> (31.03.2006)

Pomfret, Richard (1992). "The European Community's Relations with the Mediterranean Countries". In: Redmond, John (ed.). The External Relations of the European Community: The International Response to 1992. Basingstoke: Macmillan, 77-92.

Prag, Derek [n.d.]. Report drawn up on behalf of the Political Affairs Committee on Malta and its relationship with the European Community. PE 116/319/fin., Doc. A2-128/88.

Redmond, John (1993a). The Next Mediterranean Enlargement of the European Community: Turkey, Cyprus and Malta? Aldershot: Dartmouth.

Redmond, John (1993b). "The European Community and the Mediterranean Applicants: Turkey, Cyprus and Malta". In: Bank of Valletta Review, No. 7, 1-42.

Redmond, John (1994a). Prospective Europeans: New Members for the European Union. Hertfordshire: Harvester Wheatsheaf.

Redmond, John (1994b). "Cyprus and Malta: Still the Mediterranean Orphans?". In: Redmond, John (ed.). Prospective Europeans: New Members for the European Union. Hertfordshire: Harvester Wheatsheaf, 133-147.

Reiter, Erich/ Gärtner, Heinz (eds.) 2001. Small States and Alliances. Heidelberg: Physica-Verlag.

Rittberger, Volker (2005). Approaches to the Study of Foreign Policy Derived from International Relations Theories. <http://w210.ub.uni-tuebingen.de/dbt/volltexte/2005/ 1617/>, (24.04.2006)

Rittberger, Volker/ Andrei, Verena (2005). „Macht, Profit und Interessen – Auswärtige Kulturpolitik und Außenpolitiktheorien". In: Maaß, Kurt-Jürgen (ed.). Kultur und Außenpolitik. Baden-Baden: Nomos Verlagsgesellschaft, 31-52.

Rossi, Enzo (1986). Malta on the Brink. From Western Democracy to Libyan Satellite. London: Alliance Publishers for the Institute for European Defence & Strategic Studies.

Rothstein, Robert L. (1968). Alliances and Small Powers. New York: Columbia University Press.

Stratenschulte, Eckart D. [n.d.]. Die zentrale Rolle der Peripherie? http://www.europaeische-bewegung.de/fileadmin/files_ebd/PDF-Dateien/EAB_MALTA_Bericht_lang_EDS.doc, (27.07.2006)

Streeten, Paul (1993). "The Special Problems of Small Countries". In: World Development, Vol. 21, No. 2, 197-202.

Sutton, Paul (1987). "Political Aspects". In: Clarke, Colin/ Payne, Tony (eds.). Politics, Security and Development in Small States. London: Allen & Unwin, 3-25.

Tömmel, Ingeborg (2005). Das politische System der EU. München: Oldenbourg Wissenschaftsverlag.

Tzermias, Pavlos (2004). „Malta". In: Weidenfeld, Werner (ed.). Die Staatenwelt Europas. Bonn: bpb, 240-246.

Walker, Luke/ Elliott, Joy (2004). In or Out: Small Island States and the Expanding European Union. <http://www.giee.ntnu.edu.tw/island/2004_ISLANDS8_proceedings/ISISA8/017%202-2-A-2%20Joy%20Elliott%20&%20Luke%20Walker%20_Canada_pdf>, (11.04.2006)

Waltz, Kenneth N. (1979). Theory of International Politics. Reading: Addison-Wesley.

Waschkuhn, Arno (ed.) 1993. Kleinstaat: Grundsätzliche und aktuelle Probleme. Vaduz: Verlag der Liechtensteinischen Akademischen Gesellschaft.

Wendt, Alexander (1992). „Anarchy is what states make of it: the social construction of power politics". In: International Organization Volume 46, No. 2, 391-425.

Xuereb, Peter G. [n.d.]. The Draft Treaty establishing a Constitution for Europe – What it means for us. <http://home.um.edu.mt/edrc/mesa/draft_const_treaty.PDF>

Zibrandt von Dosenrode-Lynge, Sören (1993). Westeuropäische Kleinstaaten in der EG und EPZ. Zürich: Verlag Rüegger.

Official EU documents

1999 Regular Report from the Commission on Malta's Progress Towards Accession. <http://europa.eu.int/comm/enlargement/report_10_99/index.htm> (10.04. 2006)

2001 Regular Report from the Commission on Malta's Progress Towards Accession. <http://europa.eu.int/comm/enlargement/report2001/ml_en.pdf> (10.04.2006)

2002 Regular Report from the Commission on Malta's Progress Towards Accession. http://ec.europa.eu/comm/enlargement/report2002/ml_en.pdf (14.05.2006)

Briefing No. 5 Malta and Relations with the European Union. European Parliament. PE 167/350/rev. 4. Luxembourg 1st March 2000. <http://www.europarl.eu.int/ enlargement/briefings/pdf/5a1_en.pdf> (07.04.2006)

Chairman's Statement 10th Anniversary Euro-Mediterranean Summit. <http://ec. europa.eu/comm/external_relations/euromed/summit1105/chairmans_statement.pdf> (03.08.2006)

Commission recommendation on the 2004 update of the Broad Guidelines of the Economic Policies of the Member States and the Community (for the 2003-2005 period). 7.4.2004.COM (2004) 238. <http://ec.europa.eu/economy_finance/publications/european_economy/2004/comm2004_238en.pdf> (20.05.2006)

Comprehensive monitoring report on Malta's preparations for membership. <http://europa.eu.int/comm/enlargement/report_2003/pdf/cmr_mt_final.pdf> (10.05. 2006)

Council Regulation (EC) No 555/2000 of 13 March 2000 on the implementation of operations in the framework of the pre-accession strategy for the Republic of Cyprus and the Republic of Malta, <http://ec.europa.eu/comm/enlargement/arch_countries/malta/pdf/555-2000-130300.pdf> (25.07.2006)

Country Profile Malta. <http://www.europarl.europa.eu/enlargement_new/applicants/pdf/malta_profile_en.pdf> (11.05.2006)

The Euro-Mediterranean Partnership. External Relations, <http://ec.europa.eu/ comm/xternal_relations/euromed/index.htm> (03.08.2006)

Europe and the challenge of enlargement, 24 June 1992. Bulletin of the European Communities, Supplement 3/92 <http://aei.pitt.edu/1573/01/challenge_of_enlargement_June_92.pdf>, (06.05.2006)

European Parliament. Report on enlargement: progress report. Motion for a resolution. A5-0371/2002. PE 320.209. November 2002, <http://www.europarl.europa.eu/omk/sipade3?PUBREF=-//EP//NONSGML+REPORT+A5-2002-0371+0+DOC+WORD+V0//EN&L=EN&LEVEL=2&NAV=S&LSTDOC=Y> (14.05.2006)

Resolution on Malta and its relationship with the European Community. Official Journal of the European Communities, No C 262/144, Doc. A2-128/88.

The challenge of enlargement. Commission opinion on Malta's application for membership, Bulletin of the European Communities, Supplement 4/93. <http://aei.pitt.edu/5761/01/003723_1.pdf> (12.05.2006)

SCADPlus: The 2004 enlargement: the challenge of a 25-member-EU. <http://europa.eu.int/scadplus/leg/en/lvb/e50017.htm> (11.05.2006)

Internet sources

Malta Government Documents

http://docs.justice.gov.mt/lom/legislation/english/leg/vol_1/chapt0.pdf Constitution of Malta. (16.06.2006)

http://mfin.gov.mt/image.aspx?site=NECC&ref=Euro%20Strategy%20Doc Government of Malta / Central Bank of Malta. Malta's strategy for participating in economic and monetary union and adopting the Euro (05.08.2006)

http://www.doi.gov.mt/EN/elections/default.asp, Department of Information, Malta. General Election Results. (27.06.2006)

http://www.doi.gov.mt/EN/islands/lists/list6.asp, Department of Information, Malta. Prime Ministers. (28.06.2006)

http://www.foreign.gov.mt/pages.aspx?page=48, External Affairs Directorate, Malta. (27.07.2006)

http://www.foreign.gov.mt/showdoc.aspx?id=96&filesource=4&file=ILLEGal%20Im migrants.pdf Ministry of Foreign Affairs, Malta Speaking Notes on Illegal Immigration to Malta, 5th July 2005. (04.08.2006)

http://www.foreign.gov.mt/showdoc.aspx?id=210&filesource=4&file=press%20release%20Hungarian%20FM%20300606.pdf Ministry of Foreign Affairs, Press release 30th June: EU lacks real commitment for Malta's illegal immigration problem. (04.08.2006) http://www.foreign.gov.mt/showdoc.aspx?id=210&filesource=4&file=Press%20Release%2017%20July%202006%20Internaltional%20Media.pdf, Press release: Foreign Minister raises illegal immigration with resident EU Ambassadors. (03.08.2006)

http://www.gov.mt/frame.asp?l=2&url=http://www.doi.gov.mt, Referendum Final Results. (19.07.2006)

http://www.gov.mt/frame.asp?l=2&url=http://www.doi.gov.mt/en/pmspchs/default.asp, Speech by the Prime Minister, the Hon Lawrence Gonzi, at Chatman House, London, entitled "The Challenges of Convergence", 2nd June, 2006. (04.08.2006)

Other Internet Sources

http://www.delmlt.cec.eu.int/eu_assistance/financial_cooperation.htm, Representation of the European Commission in Malta (26.07.2006)

http://www.eic.de/fileadmin/user_upload/Malta.pdf Country Profile Fact Sheet Malta. (11.05.2006)

http://www.epp-ed.org/Press/pdoc03/accession_treaty-mt.doc, Group of the European People's Party (Christian Democrats) and European Democrats in the European Parliament (EPP-ED), Malta Accession Treaty. (13.07.2006)

http://www.euractiv.com/en/constitution/eu-presidencies/article-138197, EU Presidencies. (22.07.2006)

http://www.maltanetworkresources.com/modules/maltadir/visit.php?cid=125&lid=216&PHPSESSID=ad2f5da76b12089ef40ea806c669b7e7, BBC News, September 6, 1998. (05.07.2006)

http://www.mic.org.mt/Malta-EU/NPAA%20Final%202002.doc, Malta: National Programme for the Adoption of the Acquis (NPAA), January 2002. (04.04.2006)

http://www.mfat.govt.nz/foreign/regions/europe/countrypapers/malta.html, Key Facts of Malta by New Zealand Ministry of Foreign Affairs and Trade. (12.05.2006)

http://www.mic.org.mt/AGGORNAT/general/aggornat_spec_edition.htm, Aġġornat, Weekly bulletin published by the Malta-EU Information Centre, No. 156, December 2002 (13.05.2006)

http://www.nso.gov.mt/statdoc/document_file.aspx?id=118, National Statistics Office Malta: Benchmarking Malta in Europe (14.05.2006)

Appendix

List of Abbreviations

CEECs Central and Eastern European Countries

EC European Community

ECJ European Court of Justice

ECSC European Coal and Steal Community

EEC European Economic Community

EFTA European Free Trade Association

ENP European Neighbourhood Policy

EPC European Political Cooperation

EU European Union

EU-15 EU member states before enlargement round in 2004 (Austria, Belgium, Denmark, Finland, France, Germany, Great Britain, Greece, Ireland, Italy, Luxembourg, Netherlands, Portugal, Spain, Sweden)

EURATOM European Atomic Energy Community

FDI Foreign Direct Investment

GDP Gross Domestic Product

GMP Global Mediterranean Policy

GWU General Workers' Union

IGC Intergovernmental Conference

MEP Member of the European Parliament

MLP Malta Labour Party

MP Member of Parliament

NAM Non-Aligned Movement

NECC National Euro Changeover Committee

NPAA National Programme for the Adoption of the *acquis*

PN Nationalist Party

SEA Single European Act

SMEs Small and Medium-Sized Enterprises

TEC Treaty Establishing the European Economic Community

UNCTAD United Nations Conference on Trade and Development

Series Subscription

Please enter my subscription to the *Interdisciplinary Series of the Centre for Intercultural and European Studies*, ISSN 1865-2255, edited by Gudrun Hentges, Volker Hinnenkamp, Anne Honer, Hans-Wolfgang Platzer, as follows:

❒ complete series

starting with

❒ volume # 1

❒ volume # ___

  ❒ please also include the following volumes: #___, ___, ___, ___, ___, ___,

❒ the next volume being published

  ❒ please also include the following volumes: #___, ___, ___, ___, ___, ___,

❒ 1 copy per volume   OR   ❒ ___ copies per volume

Subscription within Germany:

You will receive every volume at 1st publication at the regular bookseller's price – incl. s & h and VAT.

Payment:

❒ Please bill me for every volume.

❒ Lastschriftverfahren: Ich/wir ermächtige(n) Sie hiermit widerruflich, den Rechnungsbetrag je Band von meinem/unserem folgendem Konto einzuziehen.

Kontoinhaber: ______________________ Kreditinstitut: ______________________

Kontonummer: ______________________ Bankleitzahl: ______________________

International Subscription:

Payment (incl. s & h and VAT) in advance for

❒ 10 volumes/copies (€ 319.80)   ❒ 20 volumes/copies (€ 599.80)

❒ 40 volumes/copies (€ 1,099.80)

Please send my books to:

NAME ______________________ DEPARTMENT ______________________

ADDRESS ____

POST/ZIP CODE ______________________ COUNTRY ______________________

TELEPHONE ______________________ EMAIL ______________________

date/signature ____

Please fax to: **0511 / 262 2201 (+49 511 262 2201)**
or mail to: *ibidem*-Verlag, Julius-Leber-Weg 11, D-30457 Hannover,Germany
or send an e-mail: ibidem@ibidem-verlag.de

***ibidem*-Verlag**
Melchiorstr. 15
D-70439 Stuttgart
info@ibidem-verlag.de
www.ibidem-verlag.de
www.edition-noema.de
www.autorenbetreuung.de

Zeitfracht Medien GmbH
Ferdinand-Jühlke-Straße 7
99095 Erfurt, Deutschland
produktsicherheit@kolibri360.de